Sentence Strategies for Multilingual Learners

This book presents Combinations as a set of high-yield instructional strategies for advancing academic literacy for multilingual learners and all students. It discusses the strategies themselves as well as how they work to advance content and language learning simultaneously, across the grades and content areas.

The book is particularly beneficial for all teachers working with linguistically and culturally diverse learners to accelerate their language and content learning. Utilizing these strategies will not only greatly improve students' writing but also supports their critical thinking, content area reading and language comprehension skills. This book argues for utilizing Combinations with Strategic Inquiry, presenting evidence of how each amplifies the impact of the other, and how together they address many of the challenges to learning new and counter-cultural methods and to establishing school and district cultures in support of multilingual learners' success.

This book is a great resource for classroom teachers, literacy coaches and school and district administrators who want to support multilingual learners and all students to thrive.

Nell Scharff Panero is an associate professor of educational leadership in the School of Education at Hunter College, City University of New York and the former director of the Center for Educational Leadership at Baruch College, City University of New York.

Joanna Yip is a multilingual learner instructional specialist in New York City. She has worked in the field of education as a teacher, college counselor, instructional and leadership coach and consultant on specific projects focusing on multilingual learners.

Other Eye on Education Books

Available from Routledge
(www.routledge.com/eyeoneducation)

The Classroom Teacher's Guide to Supporting English Language Learners
Pamela Mesta and Olga Reber

Vocabulary Strategies that Work, Second Edition Do This—Not That!
Lori Wilfong

Your World Language Classroom: Strategies for In-Person and Digital Instruction
Rachelle Dené Poth

Differentiated Instruction: A Guide for World Language Teachers, 3rd Edition
Deborah Blaz

The World Language Teacher's Guide to Active Learning: Strategies and Activities for Increasing Student Engagement, 2nd Edition
Deborah Blaz

An Educator's Guide to Dual Language Instruction: Increasing Achievement and Global Competence, K–12
Gayle Westerberg and Leslie Davison

Determining Difference from Disability: What Culturally Responsive Teachers Should Know
Gerry McCain and Megan Farnsworth

Remote Teaching and Learning in the Elementary ELA Classroom Instructional Strategies and Best Practices
Sean Ruday and Jennifer Cassidy

Remote Teaching and Learning in the Middle and High ELA Classroom Instructional Strategies and Best Practices
Sean Ruday and Jennifer Cassidy

Sentence Strategies for Multilingual Learners

Advancing Academic Literacy through Combinations

Nell Scharff Panero and Joanna Yip

Routledge
Taylor & Francis Group
NEW YORK AND LONDON

Designed cover image: © Getty images

First published 2024
by Routledge
605 Third Avenue, New York, NY 10158

and by Routledge
4 Park Square, Milton Park, Abingdon, Oxon, OX14 4RN

Routledge is an imprint of the Taylor & Francis Group, an informa business

© 2024 Nell Scharff Panero and Joanna Yip

The right of Nell Scharff Panero and Joanna Yip to be identified as author of this work has been asserted in accordance with sections 77 and 78 of the Copyright, Designs and Patents Act 1988.

All rights reserved. No part of this book may be reprinted or reproduced or utilised in any form or by any electronic, mechanical, or other means, now known or hereafter invented, including photocopying and recording, or in any information storage or retrieval system, without permission in writing from the publishers.

Trademark notice: Product or corporate names may be trademarks or registered trademarks, and are used only for identification and explanation without intent to infringe.

ISBN: 978-1-032-25086-1 (hbk)
ISBN: 978-1-032-22849-5 (pbk)
ISBN: 978-1-003-28147-4 (ebk)

DOI: 10.4324/9781003281474

Typeset in Palatino
by SPi Technologies India Pvt Ltd (Straive)

For Anabel, Nell's greatest teacher.

For Agnes, Joanna's mother, who wanted to be an educator of immigrant children herself but never got the chance. 獻給葉天恩的媽媽，葉陳紫娟。早年移民美國，她一直希望成為移民兒童的教育家，可惜沒有機會

Contents

Meet the Authors ix
Foreword x
Acknowledgments xiv

PART I What We Are Proposing 1

1 Introduction 3

2 Combinations for Multilingual Learners 11

3 Combinations + Strategic Inquiry: Closing the
   Research–Implementation Gap for Multilingual
   Learners 28

PART II Getting into the Work 45

4 Sentence Boundaries 47

5 Hook It Up, Set It Up: The Power of Conjunctions 69

6 Stretch It: Expansion, Appositives, Combining
   and Parallel Revision 92

7 Design and Teaching Tips: Multilingual Entry Points
   for Combinations 114

PART III   What It Looks Like on the Ground 135

8 A Case Study (The Nitty Gritty of the What,
   How and to What Effect) 137

9 Call to Action 166

   Appendix A. 170
   Appendix B. 171

Meet the Authors

Nell Scharff Panero is an associate professor of educational leadership in the School of Education at Hunter College, CUNY and the former director of the Center for Educational Leadership at Baruch College, CUNY. While at Baruch, she co-developed the strategic inquiry model of school improvement and has led, trained facilitators in and studied multiple iterations of this work. Most recently, she led implementation of *Writing is Thinking through Strategic Inquiry (WITsi)* in NYC's most struggling "renewal" high schools. Dr. Panero is a former high school English teacher and has a PhD in Education from New York University. She is the author of numerous publications, including *Getting the maximum from the minimum: An adaptive system for scaling school reform* (*Leadership and Policy in Schools*, 2019) and *Strategic Inquiry: Starting Small for Big Results in Education* (with J.E. Talbert), Harvard Education Press, 2013.

Joanna Yip is a multilingual learner instructional specialist in New York City. She has worked in the field of education as a teacher, college counselor, instructional and leadership coach and consultant on specific projects focusing on multilingual learners. Her projects include programs that develop literacy of students with interrupted formal education (SIFE), reading intervention programs for diverse learners in general education settings with a focus on ELs and biliteracy and serving as an instructor in teacher preparation programs. Dr. Yip has a Master's degree in TESOL from Hunter College, a doctorate in urban education policy from the CUNY Graduate Center and a school building leadership credential from the New York City Leadership Academy.

Foreword

In *Sentence Strategies for Multilingual Learners: Advancing Academic Literacy through Combinations*, Nell Scharff Panero and Joanna Yip make the case for an instructional approach that simultaneously builds literacy skills, content knowledge and metalinguistic awareness. The approach they propose explicitly instruction focused on the microcosm of sentence and progressive mastery through deliberate practice – is elegantly approachable and immediately actionable. Paired with structured Strategic Inquiry, a professional learning approach that supports sustained inquiry, reflection and teacher collaboration, what they offer in this book has the potential of being a game changer for K-12 teachers and their multilingual students. Imagine a generation of teachers across the content areas equipped with knowledge of how to demystify how the English language works in academic texts and the skills to support their students to use this metalinguistic awareness to craft their own effective texts. Undoubtedly, this would lead to increased academic outcomes for multilingual (and other) students and also eliminate a great deal of frustration and stress for students and teachers alike. Knowledge is power, and knowledge of language gives educators and their students the superpower to read texts critically and create texts intentionally to achieve specific goals.

Panero and Yip recognize they are making a bold claim in this book: that small instructional shifts using a set of sentence-level instructional activities can build students' proficiency in writing, reading comprehension, content knowledge, knowledge of the English language and analytical thinking – all at once. At first glance, this assertion may be hard to believe. But a closer examination reveals that, although the focus is on analyzing sentences, like an iceberg, a lot more is going on under the surface. Readers will make their own discoveries, but here is what struck me as a few of the potential benefits of the *Combinations* approach:

- **Integrated content, language and literacy**: Research suggests that language and literacy instruction is most effective, not to mention efficient, when embedded in intellectually engaging content learning and that multilingual learners need sustained opportunities to explore and use language for meaningful academic purposes. By zooming in on sentences in the academic texts students are actually reading in the content areas, students are given the opportunity to deepen their content knowledge at the same time as they develop their linguistic skills.
- **Metalinguistic awareness building**: Research also has demonstrated that investing adequate time to support multilingual students to build metalinguistic awareness, or knowledge about "how language works" to achieve specific purposes, can lead to a big payoff. When students become curious about, notice, discuss and think critically about how writers craft effective sentences by using patterns of language to appeal to their intended audiences and express their ideas clearly, they are more informed language users and can apply this "meta" awareness to their own writing. Metalinguistic awareness also supports students' reading comprehension of complex texts because they are already acclimated to pause while reading to analyze language patterns and the meanings embedded within them.
- **Potential for transfer**: Once students develop the analytical skills for understanding how sentences work, they can transfer this knowledge to other "chunks" of language. The mere act of exploring sentences, with curiosity and inquiry about the meaning of the language patterns encountered, can transfer to more discrete chunks of language (i.e., clause, phrase and word level) and larger chunks of language (i.e., paragraph, section and whole text level). Once students learn to see how language works, they can't unsee it.

Teachers want to develop sophisticated linguistic knowledge and engage their students in language exploration activities that will advance both literacy and content knowledge development, but without opportunities to learn from experts and the peer support needed to grow, facilitating these activities can be challenging to implement. This book provides a manageable starting point: by trying out the sentence-level strategies in this book and engaging in collaborative inquiry with their peers, teachers can build students' language knowledge and skills and, at the same time, build their own knowledge and skills.

Traditional (and still widely used) methods of language teaching – namely instruction that focuses on identifying parts of speech, memorizing grammar rules and filling out worksheets in isolation from content learning – is what most of us endured in school, and it tends to be both boring and unsuccessful in terms of impact on student learning. It may even cause students to detest language learning. Panero and Yip offer an alternative approach that is highly respectful of both teachers and multilingual students, as it positions each group as intellectually capable of complex work.

Some may worry that this type of teaching is too complex for content area teachers. What these naysayers may be forgetting is that teachers are brilliant professionals and, by nature of their vocation, are life-long learners. They can do this. But they need the support to do so. One of the great failings of our educational system is to have high expectations for multilingual learners without providing teachers with the necessary preparation, ongoing professional learning, instructional materials and systems to support *their* success. As Panero and Yip point out, teachers are doing the best they can with the tools they've been given. When they are denied opportunities to learn and grow, teachers of multilingual learners feel underprepared, unsupported and largely ineffectual. We should have high expectations of our teachers, but we shouldn't expect them to "sink or swim" on their own. This book and the instructional and professional learning approaches for which it advocates are a step in the right direction of providing our teachers the respect and support they need to excel.

Success leads to a feeling of empowerment and cultivates motivation for students and teachers alike. Using this book with their colleagues in a culture of learning and sustained inquiry, teachers will feel empowered because they will know how to help students navigate their own language development and have the tools to identify students' strengths and areas of growth. Multilingual students will feel empowered as they learn to "crack the code" of the hidden language of academic texts and develop the skills to use language to achieve their goals and reach their full potential.

Pamela Spycher, PhD, WestEd

Acknowledgments

We are grateful to Michelle Brochu, Senior WITsi Consultant and professional developer extraordinaire, who has taught the strategies we promote in this book to thousands of teachers with a passion and skill that is unmatched. Thank you, Michelle, for making this work so much better by always figuring out the very best ways to teach it. We are grateful to Felicia Hirata, an invaluable partner always. We are grateful to the extraordinary leaders who have been our co-conspirators, especially Deirdre DeAngelis for piloting the marriage of Combinations and Strategic Inquiry (SI) and Aimee Horowitz and Elif Gure (in New York City) and Amy Gottesfeld (in San Francisco) for teaching us what it takes to bring Combinations plus SI to scale.

We thank Luis Quan for believing right away and connecting us with the legendary Eva Garcia. In her role as Executive Director of the NYC Regional Bilingual Education Resource Network (RBERN) at Fordham University, Eva supported us and spread the word to Angel Rodriguez of the English Language Learner Consortium and Carlos Sanchez and his amazing team at the Hudson Valley RBERN. They in turn introduced us to other fierce EL advocates, including Tiara Reyes-Vega, Diane Howitt, Tanya Rosado-Barringer, Yanira Stoker and June Wai. We are indebted to you all for your partnership and support.

We are grateful to the many other district leaders, principals, assistant principals, coaches, teachers, students and facilitators with whom we have collaborated over the years and from whom we have learned more than we can say, especially Hongying Shen, Joanna Cohen-Malament, Rachael Wasilewski-Alcantara, Beverly Guity, Karyna Tejeda, Mark Anderson, Cyndi Kerr, Michael Alcoff, Eileen Coppola, Lilliana Vendra, Isabella Robertson, Ilia Edwards, Vivian Selenikas, Monica Brady, Esther Shali-Ogli, Tyee Chin, Dan Scanlon, Rodney Arthur, Neil Ganesh, Tara O'Brien, Kimmerly Nieves, Paul Wilbur, Breina Lampert,

Harpreet Overstreet, Julie Bingay-Lopez, Allyson Ambrose; Lilliam Katcher, Allison Krenn, Lydia Abogaida, Daniel Garretson, Camille Stephens, Leo Smith, Don Neubauer, Grace Oh, Katie Ottiavani, Laura Pamplona, Nina Reed, Fatima Flores, Laura Rivera, Laura Blacklund, Julie Skiddell, Christine Wallace, Damen Davis, Datona Bradley, Stephanie Khoury, Sesaley Graciani, Rosa Rivera-McCutchen, Sandy Yark, Helen Murray, Viviana Toure, Laura Tavarez, Randy Diaz, Roderigo Salaz, Miguel Antunes, Lisa Auslander, David Neagley, Melissa Jacobs, Emily Erler, Emily Dentinger, Nicole Charette Santora, Lina Adinyayev and Erin Stark.

Ros Cooper and Bob Davies, thank you for the song.

Caroline Chauncey, thank you for encouraging this book. At Routledge, we thank Karen Adler, Justin Lee, Megha Patel and Divya Muthu for taking good care of us. William Waters, thank you for helping us zoom in on academic literacy and for keeping the writing flowing. We thank Carrie Lane for her expert editing. And we are beyond grateful to Michelle Maher, the best project manager in the universe, for keeping us on track from start to finish.

We thank Alice Cohen and Lisa Bambino, wonderful teachers for Anabel, and for Nell.

To Doug and Anabel, thank you for your patience, and for always being in Nell's corner. Doug, you are Nell's favorite editor. You always get it.

To Dariana Castro, Dennis Caindec and Melissa de Leon, who are Joanna's dearest and most beloved colleagues who have journeyed with her as educators for multilingual learners since the start.

Part I
What We Are Proposing

1

Introduction

Despite the urgent need to better serve multilingual learners in the United States, there is an unacceptable gap between current teaching and leadership practices and those needed to change the status quo. We hope this book will make a new and important contribution toward closing that gap. We argue that a small set of sentence-level literacy strategies we call *Combinations* is a powerful way to dramatically improve not only language development and academic performance for multilingual learners, but teacher and leadership practice as well.

Among all multilingual learners (a group that encompasses many groups of linguistically diverse students whose home language is not English), students who are designated as English Learners (EL) based on English language proficiency assessments are the fastest-growing student population nationwide (Kena et al., 2014), and there is an increasing focus on improving outcomes for these students, including federal regulations holding states accountable for improving English language proficiency (see Mathewson, 2016). Yet, school systems have not delivered on their responsibility to provide a comparable and adequate education for these linguistically minoritized students. Achievement outcomes for students who are designated as EL remain stubbornly poor, and the disproportionality between EL and non-EL performance on most metrics of academic achievement remains high. According to the 2022 National Assessment for Educational Progress results (NAEP), 32% of eighth-grade

ELs performed at or above the NAEP basic level in Reading compared to 73% of non-EL eighth-grade students (NAEP Report Card: Reading, 2022). In mathematics, 24% of eighth-grade ELs performed at or above the NAEP basic level compared to 65% of non-EL students (NAEP Report Card: Mathematics, 2022). While only 28% of non-EL students in the 12th grade performed at or above the proficient level in writing, the percentage of EL writing at or above the proficient level was an abysmal 1% (The Nation's Report Card, 2011)!

Multilingual learners, like all students, must now reach a higher bar than ever before in order to meet more challenging standards and to graduate from high school and college career and community ready. There is consensus among EL experts that a "reformulation of practice" (Heritage et al., 2015) is required to get them there. This reformulation, most experts agree, requires (1) that all teachers share responsibility for improving outcomes for multilingual learners; this is no longer the realm of only the English Language Development (ELD) teacher; (2) that teachers must integrate language and content instruction in order to develop critical thinking, and that language instruction is most effective when embedded in disciplinary practices; and (3) that all multilingual learners must be given sustained opportunities to practice and use language for meaningful academic purposes (Adger et al., 2019; Gibbons, 2014; Walqui, 2006).

While this vision for reformulating practice is beginning to take hold in conversations among educators, it is not yet taking hold in practice. To significantly change both performance outcomes for multilingual learners and teacher and leadership practice within school systems, the field needs a different approach. Our book argues that a focus on Combinations is one powerful way to enable teachers, leaders and school communities to bring about this needed change.

In mathematics, a *combination* is one of several possible variations in which a set or number of things can be ordered or arranged. In this book, we present Combinations as a set of sentence-level literacy strategies that, when implemented collectively and intentionally, comprise a powerful approach for advancing academic literacies for multilingual learners. The strategies teach students language forms that operate at the level of the sentence and how they can be manipulated and adjusted to convey varied, nuanced meanings. Because they develop students' ability to comprehend shades of meaning as expressed in varied language forms and skillfully manipulate these forms as communicators of nuanced and precise meanings about academic content, we call this collection of strategies Combinations.

While Combinations is powerful for all students, it is particularly needed and impactful for students who are learning English because the strategies teach students how the English language works in the small and thus accessible microcosm of the sentence. They do so while also teaching comprehension and expression (oral and written), always embedded within, never separate and apart from, disciplinary content. By doing many things at once within the contained and accessible structure of the sentence, Combinations provides a practical and efficient way to help build and sustain a teaching force to meet the challenge of the moment: high levels of discipline-based academic literacies for all.

We understand that our argument is counterintuitive. *Can focusing on something as small as the sentence really yield such tremendous results?* Our conviction is grounded in over 30 years of our collective experience and in the results of independent research of two iterations of an inquiry-based school reform called strategic inquiry (SI), which included a focus on these sentence strategies and was found to dramatically improve student and school performance (Talbert et al., 2012; Wohlstetter et al., 2018). The findings from this research provide evidence that it is possible to help close both the research–practice gap and the gap in academic literacy outcomes for multilingual learners by focusing on a few high-leverage areas for change: powerful sentence-level literacy and thinking routines used with academic content paired with structured collaborative inquiry. This pairing of Combinations and SI leads to consistently impactful results not only for multilingual learners but also for teaching, organizational change and leadership practice.

The strategies we lay out address three significant needs in literacy instruction. First, system leaders and policymakers seek to make sizeable shifts in teacher and administrator understanding and practice in terms of how to teach literacy. Their recommendations are based on two decades of empirical research on supporting multilingual learners with academic literacy (e.g., National Reading Panel (2000); National Literacy Panel on Language-Minority Children and Youth (August & Shanahan, 2006)), most of which has failed to make its way into the classroom. Our strategies help address this research–practice gap. Second, while there is a substantial research base about reading that is now penetrating the national discourse and beginning to impact practice generally (see Hanford, 2018; Luscombe, 2022), (a) there is a dearth of research about writing as compared with reading (Graham & Perin, 2007) and (b) little attention has been paid to what recent literacy reform efforts mean for students who are developing literacy in English as a new language (Escamilla et al., 2022; Graham et al., 2019; Graham & Perin, 2007). Thus, there are gaps in the research that our strategies also address. Finally, the field is struggling to design assessment systems that tell teachers precisely what their multilingual learners know and can do in both language and content that also consider the students' home language. We will show how Combinations can form the basis of an assessment system that provides key information needed to better understand the assets and needs of multilingual learners in a manner that is efficient, manageable and actionable.

Our strategies also address significant needs in educational leadership. While there is a strong empirical basis indicating *what* is needed to improve teaching and learning for multilingual learners, there are few research-based models that show leaders *how* to lead the change in schools and school systems (Talbert, 2014). Leaders need a model of implementation that anticipates and addresses both technical and cultural challenges to change (the extent of new learning that will be required and the resistance likely entailed in reformulating practice). Our theory grows out of and incorporates a model of professional learning that does just that (Panero & Talbert, 2013). By showing how Combinations, when paired with SI, develops buy-in, new beliefs and needed skills among teachers, we make clear a proven path for implementation (Wohlstetter et al., 2018). We argue that a tight focus on Combinations can rapidly improve the performance of multilingual learners and galvanize teacher team members' collective efficacy as both teachers and leaders of change.

In this book, you will learn not only about the instructional strategies comprising Combinations, which we have found are critical in supporting multilingual learners to develop academic literacies, but also how they have made an impact on teachers and schools. **Part I** makes clear what we are proposing and why. In Chapter 2, we define Combinations and show its benefits for students, teachers and leaders. We present our argument for how and why our approach addresses significant needs in the field. In Chapter 3, we describe the problems in practice that teachers face in developing academic literacy for multilingual learners and explain how Combinations plus SI addresses many of these challenges.

In **Part II**, the core of our book, we explain in detail the seven strategies comprising Combinations. We group the strategies according to their function – those that support an understanding of sentence basics or "boundaries" (Chapter 4); those that teach students to "hook up" or "set up" ideas within a sentence (Chapter 5) and those that teach students to "stretch" their ideas (Chapter 6).[1] In each of these three chapters, we describe the core language function addressed; what students need to learn to develop academic literacy; the gaps in teacher practice that this set of strategies is designed to address and how, precisely, the strategies work to close these gaps. We include examples from multiple grade levels and content areas, hoping to make our point persuasively that each strategy is applicable broadly. We describe how each strategy is designed, how it is taught and how teachers can differentiate tasks, drawing upon multilingual entry points, to allow access to rigorous content regardless of a student's current level of English language proficiency. In Chapter 7, we take a deeper dive into the multilingual entry points. Overall, our goal in Part II is to demystify Combinations – making it clear *how* to design and implement these strategies and *why* doing so is so incredibly worthwhile.

Part III features an extended case study of learning and leading the work from the perspective of a teacher (Chapter 8). We highlight how Combinations plus SI works to develop students' academic literacies as well as student and teacher confidence. We show how the strategies can be embedded in adult development systems so that they can truly take hold in school communities. We end with a call to action (Chapter 9).

Although our careers have followed different paths, we come together in our conviction that the strategies we present in this book represent game-changing and largely missing knowledge in the field, knowledge with the power to transform teaching and learning for and beyond multilingual learners. We hope that this book will help more teachers, leaders and researchers to think so too.

Note

1 We are indebted to Ros Cooper and the team at PS 303 in the Bronx, New York, for categorizing the strategies according to their function (*hook it up*, *set it up* and *stretch* it) and for giving us permission to use their naming of the categories in this book. To listen to "Sophisticate It", an original song, written, sung and recorded by Ros' brother-in-law, Bob Davies, and used to introduce the strategies to elementary students at PS 303, see https://strategicinquiry.com/sophisticate-it/.

References

Adger, C. T., Snow, C. E., & Christian, D. (Eds.). (2019). *What teachers need to know about language.* (2nd ed). Multilingual Matters.

August, D., & Shanahan, T. (2006). *Developing literacy in second-language learners: Report of the national literacy panel on language-minority children and youth.* Center for Applied Linguistics. Lawrence Erlbaum Associates.

Escamilla, K., Olsen, L., & Slavick, J. (2022). *Towards comprehensive effective literacy policy and instruction for emergent bilingual/English learner students* [White paper]. National Committee for Effective Literacy.

https://secureservercdn.net/50.62.174.75/v5e.685.myftpupload.com/wp-content/uploads/2022/04/21018-NCEL-Effective-Literacy-White-Paper-FINAL_v2.0.pdf

Gibbons, P. (2014). *Scaffolding language, scaffolding learning: Teaching English language learners in the mainstream classroom.* (2nd ed). Heinemann.

Graham, S., MacArthur, C. A., & Hebert, M. (Eds.). (2019) *Best practices in writing instruction* (3rd ed.). Guilford Press.

Graham, S., & Perin, D. (2007). *Writing next: Effective strategies to improve writing of adolescents in middle and high schools - A report to Carnegie corporation of New York.* Alliance for Excellent Education.

Hanford, E. (2018). Hard words: Why aren't kids being taught to read? *APM Reports.* https://www.apmreports.org/episode/2018/09/10/hard-words-why-american-kids-arent-being-taught-to-read

Heritage, M., Walqui, A., & Linquanti, R. (2015). *English language learners and the new standards: Developing language content knowledge and analytical practices in the classroom.* Harvard Education Press.

Kena, G., Aud, S., Johnson, F., Wang, X., Zhang, J., Rathbun, A., Wilkinson-Flicker, S., & Kristapovich, P. (2014). The condition of education 2014. NCES 2014-083. *National Center for Education Statistics.* https://nces.ed.gov/pubs2014/2014083.pdf

Luscombe, B. (2022, August 11). Inside the massive effort to change the way kids are taught to read. *Time.* https://time.com/6205084/phonics-science-of-reading-teachers/

Mathewson, T. G. (2016, Oct. 18). 4 ways ESSA will change how schools serve ell students. *K-12Dive.* https://www.k12dive.com/news/4-ways-essa-will-change-how-schools-serve-ell-students/428266/

NAEP Report Card: Mathematics. (2022). *National achievement-level results: Lower percentage of eighth-grade students at or above* NAEP Proficient *than in 2019.* The Nation's Report Card. https://www.nationsreportcard.gov/mathematics/nation/achievement/?grade=8

NAEP Report Card: Reading (2022). *National achievement-level results: Thirty-one percent of eighth-graders at or above* NAEP Proficient *in reading, lower compared to 2019.* The Nation's Report Card. https://www.nationsreportcard.gov/reading/nation/achievement/?grade=8

National Assessment of Educational Progress. (2019). *National achievement-level results*. The Nation's Report Card: Reading. https://www.nationsreportcard.gov/reading/nation/achievement/?grade=8

National Reading Panel. (2000). *Teaching children to read: An evidence-based assessment of the scientific research literature on reading and its implications for reaching instruction*. Reports of the subgroups. https://www.nichd.nih.gov/sites/default/files/publications/pubs/nrp/Documents/report.pdf

Panero, N. S., & Talbert, J. E. (2013). *Strategic inquiry: Starting small for big results in education*. Harvard Education Press.

Talbert, J. E. (2014). Aera educational change special interest group. *Lead the change series Q&A with Joan Talbert*. (40). https://www.aera.net/Portals/38/docs/SIGs/SIG155/40%20Joan%20Talbert.pdf

Talbert, J. E., Cor, M. K., Chen, P. R., Kless, L. M., & McLaughlin, M. (2012). Inquiry-based school reform: Lessons from SAM in NYC. *Center for Research on the Context of Teaching at Stanford University [Program Evaluation]*. http://www.academia.edu/29864629/Inquiry-based_School_Reform_Lessons_from_SAM_in_NYC

The Nation's Report Card (2011). *Grade 12 national results*. https://www.nationsreportcard.gov/writing_2011/g12_national.aspx?tab_id=tab1&subtab_id=Tab_8#chart

Walqui, A. (2006). Scaffolding instruction for English language learners: A conceptual framework. *International Journal of Bilingual Education and Bilingualism, 9*(2), 159–180.

Wohlstetter, P., Kim, E., & Flack, C. B. (2018). Strategic inquiry and New York City's renewal high schools. *Teachers College Columbia University, November*. https://www.tc.columbia.edu/media/news/images/2018/december/Wohlstetter_Strategic-Inquiry-Final-Report-1.0-1.pdf

2

Combinations for Multilingual Learners

The Challenge

There are approximately 5.1 million students designated as English learners (ELs) in US public schools (National Center for Educational Statistics, 2022). These students are diverse in almost every way, including country of origin, culture, the extent and nature of literacy education in their home languages and experience with learning the English language. Some of these multilingual learners have experienced quality literacy education in their primary language and are learning English, building on a strong literacy foundation. Others with limited or interrupted formal education come to the US with a much wider range of literacy-based and social and emotional needs. What many might not realize is the large number of students identified as ELs who were born in the US. Also, the majority (59%) of secondary school ELs have received six or more years of instruction in US schools without yet having reached the level of English proficiency to be reclassified (Olsen, 2010). These students are often considered to be Long-Term English Learners (LTELs). In fact, English is the third most common home language for EL students (National Center for Educational Statistics, 2022). The persistence of EL status and the disproportionate outcomes for multilingual learners across a range of metrics, however, are far

DOI: 10.4324/9781003281474-3

from inevitable. They result from the harm that we as a system have created, and therefore are reparable (Olsen, 2010). We can and must do better to support all multilingual learners.

Arguably, the greatest challenge to multilingual learners' academic success involves the failure of school systems to develop their academic literacies. All students, including multilingual learners, must now meet a higher bar for academic literacy than they have ever been expected to meet in the past. This higher bar has become a priority of federal accountability systems and curriculum standards nationwide to ensure that multilingual learners have the support needed to meet the new learning standards (Bunch et al., 2012; Quinn et al., 2012). All schools are now held accountable to do far more than helping students develop basic literacy. So, what exactly do we mean by academic literacy? What is this higher bar that all students, including multilingual learners, must now meet?

First, it may be helpful to define the term *literacy*, which has come to mean more than the ability to read and write. A more recent understanding posits a range of literacies defined by proficiency in the forms of communication central to a particular community and context (Street, 2003). Literacy therefore is social, with no one form of literacy any more inherently valuable than another; those who are literate in a particular context have command over the language and forms that allow for full participation in that community.

Academic literacy, therefore, involves the use of language and language forms needed for full participation in K-12 schooling and for college, careers and communities within a knowledge economy. The academic literacy now required of all students for these purposes involves meaningful participation and engagement with disciplinary ideas and concepts (Lesaux et al., 2016) received and communicated both orally and through print. Students are now expected to comprehend complex material across academic content areas when they read and engage with it critically. They are expected to participate in academic discourse both orally and in writing in ways that reflect disciplinary and analytical thinking. All students are expected to write, albeit in English, for a variety of purposes and audiences and with a variety of rhetorical styles:

to justify, explain, argue, propose solutions, discuss, analyze and provide reasoning (Bunch et al., 2012; Moschkovich, 2012). This is the nature of academic literacy, the literacy practices valued in and required for full participation in a school community or academic setting.

Academic literacy requires significant linguistic resources and knowledge, and is particularly challenging – and necessary – for students who are simultaneously learning to read and write in English as a new language. Multilingual learners in the US are expected to meet such high bars for academic performance and literacy in English within very short time frames. For example, in New York State, high school students who are recent arrivals to the US are required to pass English Language Arts (ELA) state exams in English in the same time frame as all other students and can only appeal this graduation requirement if they entered the US in ninth grade or after (New York State Diploma Requirements, 2022). The level of academic literacy required for success in college and careers is even more formidable. A burning question then is *how* to meet the demands of accelerating language development and academic literacies for multilingual learners.

Teachers of multilingual learners are, simply put, doing their best with what they have been provided. Those who are lucky enough to experience high-quality teacher education and professional development learn research-based best practices for supporting academic literacy for culturally and linguistically diverse students, including by building upon and developing oral language; integrating the teaching of language with content; differentiating instruction to provide access to rigor regardless of the level of English language proficiency and for valuing and drawing upon students' cultural and linguistic assets. Yet most teachers remain extremely challenged with all that is required of them: to develop high levels of academic literacy for students who have lacked access to quality instruction and therefore struggle with literacy basics; to teach language embedded within content even though they may not have been shown clearly *how* to do so; to differentiate instruction to allow access to the same rigorous instruction to all students, regardless of the level of English language proficiency and to have an asset-based (a focus on students' strengths) rather than a deficit-based (a focus on what students lack) view, even though they may have never witnessed or experienced teaching in classrooms where instruction succeeded in meeting these requirements for multilingual learners, so they may not yet truly believe in their own ability to help multilingual learners overcome their challenges and realize their innate potential.

And while research contributes much to the field's growing understanding of teaching academic literacy to multilingual learners (Lesaux et al., 2016; National Academies of Sciences, Engineering, and Medicine, 2017), how best to translate this research into practice is not always evident. Even though a teacher might keep these deficit-based questions to themselves, they might secretly wonder: *how should I prioritize among all that is being asked of me? How do I teach language with content to a high school student who is still learning to read in their home language? How do I teach and assess while drawing upon my students' full linguistic repertoires, when I don't even speak the students' home languages? How can I teach academic literacy when the students in front of me cannot write a complete sentence? How can I find the time to teach my content* and *the foundational literacy skills the students in front of me clearly need? How can I address the range of English language proficiency of the various students within my class?* The challenges can seem daunting.

A Way Forward

Multilingual learners deserve the opportunity and the resources to develop high levels of academic literacy in all the languages in their repertoire and should be supported to develop literacy in their home language as well. In this book, we present Combinations as an efficient and effective way to address many of the abovementioned challenges related to the development of academic literacy in English. Our argument is not that Combinations is *the* way to teach academic literacy but rather that it represents a critical and largely missing piece that can and should be part of a comprehensive approach to effectively serving the academic needs of multilingual learners. Combinations in a nutshell is a set of sentence-level instructional strategies through which students learn to produce and simultaneously comprehend academic meaning as it is expressed in sentences. Combinations is a set of high-yield strategies in a small and teachable format that advance academic literacies for multilingual learners to be used when the target language is English. It develops the meaning-based foundations of reading, writing and language learning in conjunction with (not separately from) academic content. It develops students' metacognitive awareness of how language works in English in ways they can apply flexibly. By working within the microcosm of the sentence, Combinations teaches the underlying understandings related to the use of widely applicable language forms that comprise academic literacies within an accessible format. A focus on language comprehension in sentences empowers multilingual learners to understand how academic literacy works in English and provides them with the foundation they need to build confidence and fluency to engage in the most demanding of academic tasks in a new language.

In "A Case for the Sentence in Reading Comprehension" (2009), Cheryl Scott describes syntax as the "workhorse" of meaning, arguing that it should be taught directly to students, given its central role in conveying meaning. We agree. Building on her ideas and those of other literacy experts regarding the critical (and largely missing) role of sentence-level instruction (Gillis & Eberhardt, 2018; Haynes et al., 2019; Hennessey, 2022; Hochman & Wexler, 2017; Sedita, 2023; Shanahan, 2022; Van Cleave, 2012; Wexler, 2022), we see Combinations as the *workhorse* of academic literacy – as an essential though by no means the only mechanism for supporting all students' ability to understand and to express academic meaning. By focusing on syntactic comprehension and awareness, Combinations supports most notably academic writing, but also many other aspects of academic literacy and also makes a significant contribution to reading comprehension (Lynch et al., 2021).

For those interested in learning about the sentence strategies comprising Combinations within the framework of a comprehensive expository writing program, we refer you to *The Writing Revolution: A Guide to Advancing Thinking through Writing in All Subjects and Grades* (Hochman & Wexler, 2017), which is an excellent companion to this book, and to our chapter footnote for professional development resources.[1] In their book, Hochman and Wexler (2017) discuss the sentence strategies presented here in the larger context of a comprehensive approach to teaching expository writing (sentence, paragraph and essay skills). Our book instead goes into detail about the sentence-level interventions specifically and their impact on academic literacy and content learning for multilingual learners in particular.

In our book, we make clear how the sentence-level activities comprising Combinations develop students' ability to comprehend shades of meaning when they read and to communicate with clarity and precision about high-level academic content when they write. Combinations includes sentence-level activities that advance students' understanding of language forms as they convey and express meaning in English. Because the strategies emphasize function, they develop students' deep understanding of how these language forms can be manipulated (variously combined) to convey nuanced and distinct meanings according to audience and purpose. This deep applied knowledge is needed for academic literacy.

Combinations: An Example

We know we are making a bold claim: that a set of small (sentence-level) activities can develop writing, reading comprehension, content knowledge and knowledge of the English language – in a word, thinking! – all at once. We illustrate our point below with an example drawn from the strategy called *expansion* (see Chapter 6).

In expansion, a teacher provides a short, simple (unexpanded) sentence about the content they have taught. This simple sentence is provided along with questions about it that a student must answer. The student then uses all the information from the simple sentence and the answers to the questions posed to construct a new "expanded" sentence. Note that in Figure 2.1, students had read and taken notes on an article about the photograph

Directions: Expand the following sentence.

Simple sentence: She took it.

"Migrant Mother"

Who?	*Dorothea Lange*
What?	*photograph "Migrant Mother"*
When?	*during the Great Depression*
Where?	*San Luis Obispo, CA*
Why?	*draw attention to the plight of migrant workers*

Expanded sentence:
During the Great Depression, Dorothea Lange took the photograph "Migrant Mother" in San Luis Obispo, California to draw attention to the plight of the migrant workers.

FIGURE 2.1 Sample of expanding sentences.
Photo by Dorothea Lange.

"Migrant Mother". This activity was used as an exit ticket (a quick check of understanding at the end of a lesson) to reinforce and assess the lesson's content while simultaneously teaching strong sentence writing. The task as provided is in bold, and the anticipated student response (the portion to be completed by students) is in italics.

Let's walk through this example to make clear how one small activity can develop students' content knowledge, writing, reading comprehension, knowledge of the English language and thinking, simultaneously. First, this activity reinforces and assesses essential content; the lesson involved reading and taking notes on a longer article, but the Combinations-based exit ticket reinforces and assesses the precise aspects of content that the teacher has identified as most important. Second, the task itself teaches how an information-rich sentence in English is crafted, breaking down for the students how discrete parts of a sentence can be put together technically as in a puzzle. It teaches this knowledge with a focus on function over grammar in the service of communicating meaning. In this example, for instance, the student has begun their expanded sentence with an answer to the question

"When?" rather than by following the order of the questions as posed in the task. The student knew that starting with "when" was an option because of an intentional instructional move by the teacher, in which the teacher explicitly taught the students this trick: that in English you can begin a sentence by answering the question "when", "where" or "why", and that doing so produces a more complex syntactic form than starting with the "who" or "what". The teacher also discussed with students whether a similar linguistic form existed in their home language. Teaching students to produce this complex form in English reinforces their understanding of the function of this linguistic structure so that students can understand it when they encounter the same structure in complex texts in English when they read. Regular practice will teach them to deploy it flexibly when they write. Lastly, the task provided students an opening to contribute their own analytical thinking, an explanation or perhaps even an inference into why the photograph was taken in a way that was integrated into the building of a detailed, information-rich sentence.

The steps of this activity, like all strategies in Combinations, provide a guided experience through which students examine closely how elements of the English language work together to communicate meaning. Students who are learning English in particular benefit from being taught explicitly how language forms in English communicate shades of meaning; their awareness of the function of particular linguistic features develops through explicit examples and explication (Knapp & Watkins, 2005), including by being asked to attend intentionally to similarities and differences between linguistic forms in English and their home language. In this "Migrant Mother" exercise, the students engage with a basic English sentence structure (she took it) and are asked to explicitly determine the placement of additional details to add meaning to the sentence. Note that they are asked to do so based on the understanding of the function of these details (by answering the question "When?") rather than through traditional grammar instruction. Students who are learning English also benefit from explicit instruction to reinforce the speech-to-print connection – in other words, multilingual learners need to be shown and told explicitly how language forms create meaning in what they read and how they can utilize the same forms in communicating meaning themselves when they write (Spycher, 2007). Learning to produce forms that will appear frequently in academic texts consolidates for students the connection between how language works in reading and writing. And the entire process is done in the context of, not divorced from, the conceptual understandings and the content students are learning. In this way, one strategic activity supports academic literacy development for all students while attending to language development for multilingual learners.

Now let's consider what the activity does for teachers working with multilingual learners. Creating this activity requires precision about the most important content and language objectives. The task provides a way to integrate the teaching of content with language and even to address writing mechanics without sacrificing content. The task provides granular formative assessment information regarding both content and skill; if a student cannot answer one or more of the questions posed (cannot supply the requested information on the dotted lines), teachers can see the specific content understanding that is missing. If the student supplies the required information on the dotted lines but then puts the information together in the constructed sentence in ways that are unclear or inaccurate, then the teacher can see which aspect of language may need to be reinforced or taught again. The task also allows for differentiation, providing all students access to the same rigorous content regardless of their level of English language proficiency; one student may expand the sentence with one question word, or a word bank can be added to support students in using the desired academic vocabulary. Another student might complete a part or all of the activity using home language.

Administrators often struggle to implement professional learning plans that integrate the needs of multilingual learners and to do so in ways that feel integrated with the teaching and learning efforts of their school or district. The use of Combinations allows administrators to organize professional learning that ties together content learning, language and literacy efforts and formative assessment in ways that address the needs of specific student groups such as multilingual learners through one set of activities for teachers. In this way, it allows for coherence. In addition, administrators are often rightly concerned with the rigor of the classroom. When using Combinations, rigor is determined by content (the complexity of the concepts and vocabulary being drawn upon and manipulated with the strategies remaining constant). This makes Combinations a heavy-hitting strategy to build students' knowledge while doing so in a concrete and doable form that simultaneously supports academic literacy and language.

How Can Small Strategies Make Such a Big Difference?

We argue that Combinations can achieve so much for students, teachers and leaders because its strategies develop most of the meaning-based language skills that make up skilled reading and writing, are fully integrated with content and address the additional considerations for students learning English – all at once and within an accessible format.

Readers may be familiar with Scarborough's Reading Rope (2001) and Sedita's Writing Rope (2019), which are powerful visual metaphors that capture research-based knowledge of the many components (or strands) that make up skilled reading and writing in English. As these ropes make clear, skilled literacy requires both code-based elements (those needed for word recognition and transcription) and meaning-based elements (those needed to access and apply a text's meaning) (Goldenberg, 2022; Lesaux et al., 2016). While Combinations does not address code-based elements of literacy, our argument is that almost all of the overlapping *meaning-based* elements needed to read and write skillfully are addressed efficiently through Combinations.

We present this argument visually in Figure 2.2. We created this figure by placing all elements from the reading and writing ropes on a Venn diagram with those that are advanced by Combinations in the center. Those elements that are *most* heavily advanced by Combinations are in bold. The code-based elements of reading and writing appear on the far left and right

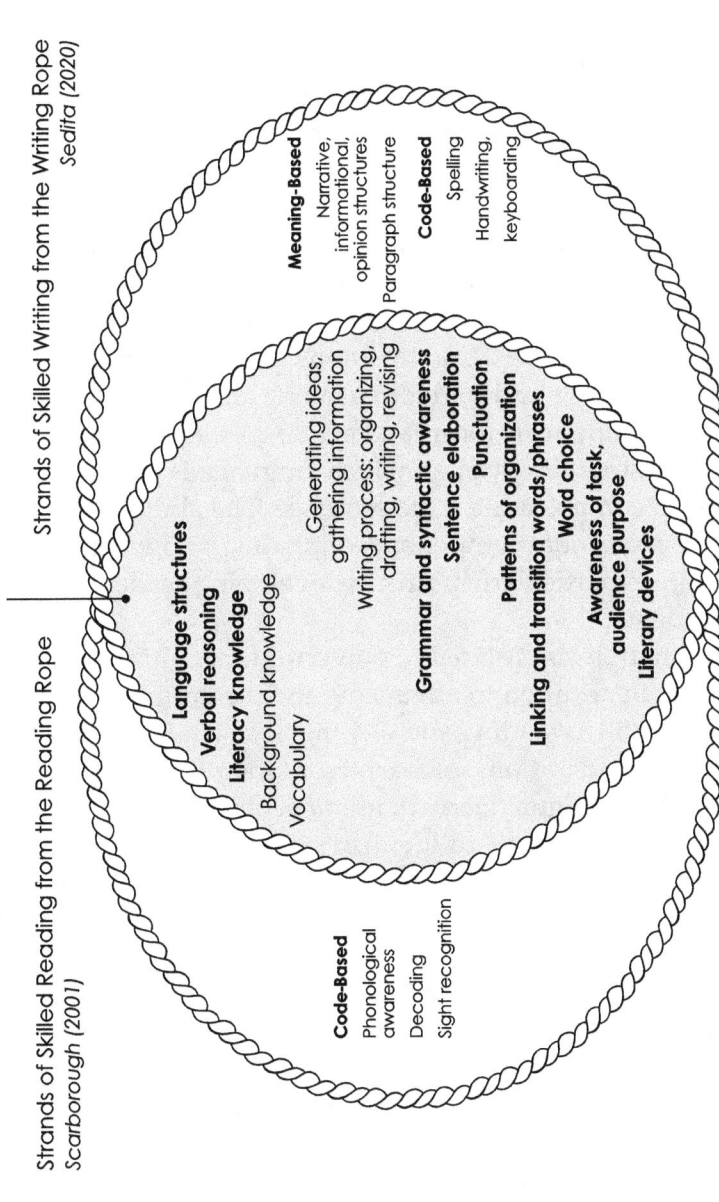

FIGURE 2.2 All skills in the shaded center of the Venn diagram are advanced through Combinations. Those in bold are most core to Combinations. Those not in bold are also advanced through Combinations, but more peripherally.

of the diagram. While critical for skilled literacy, these are not advanced through Combinations. Note also the few meaning-based elements related to writing that are not advanced through Combinations. All of the other meaning-based strands of skilled reading and writing, however, are advanced by Combinations, as shown in the shaded area in the center of the diagram.

Specifically, Combinations advances knowledge of language structure, literacy knowledge, verbal reasoning, syntactic awareness and patterns of organization and linking words and phrases – all through instruction in the microcosm of the sentence. In other words, by having students apply what they learn in terms of background knowledge and vocabulary within the provided language structures in sentences, Combinations promotes and develops literacy knowledge and verbal reasoning. It develops students' knowledge of linguistic forms and syntax as they function within the primary structure through which language is comprehended and used to communicate – the sentence. The ability to tackle so many of the essential components of reading and writing makes Combinations particularly useful in developing academic literacy for all students.

Combinations is *particularly* powerful for multilingual learners because in addition to advancing the meaning-based underpinnings of skilled reading and writing, it also takes into account additional considerations for learning academic literacy in a new language. Multilingual learners in particular benefit from direct and explicit instructions to identify similarities and differences between linguistic forms in English and their home languages and to consolidate the speech-to-print connection. Teachers of multilingual learners must take into account and draw upon students' home language literacy assets and educational histories. They must understand that some may be developing their linguistic systems in English while also developing the processes needed for literacy; and they must consider the implications of their instructional practices for students who are bilingual (Escamilla et al., 2022).

Combinations provides a concrete way to account for these considerations because it helps multilingual learners to actively make connections between English and the other linguistic systems in their repertoire. Students develop academic literacy when they understand the similarities and differences between how vocabulary, syntax and language structures work in their home language in comparison to English. Multilingual learners may construct sentences in ways that are informed by their home language. When multilingual learners develop metalinguistic awareness of how language is used in English and in their home language, they develop their understanding of the impact of linguistic choices on meaning, communication and how to address specific audiences. Hence, Combinations creates natural opportunities for metalinguistic reflection and thinking through clear tasks that require students to use language in concrete ways that promote cross-linguistic comparison. It calls their attention to the way English works very explicitly and then creates an opportunity for students to see the similarities and differences. Such metalinguistic awareness accelerates English language development and can also be a major contributor to biliteracy.

In addition, because the strategies build upon one another in a system, Combinations teaches linguistic and syntactical knowledge in connection with function in a scaffolded, recursive and gradual way. The language exploration often promoted by researchers is necessary but hard for teachers to do systematically and intentionally without deliberate planning within the context of the broader curriculum and a clear assessment of what students need to learn next. Combinations eases some of the practical challenges for teachers by offering a set of high-impact language exploration activities within a system that is directly connected to the content they are teaching.

Through Combinations, teachers can support all linguistically diverse students and especially those identified as ELs by providing explicit teaching on how academic literacy works in the context of meaning-making, content and communication for varied audiences and purposes. Knowledge of language structure and syntax enables multilingual learners to not only comprehend a text but also to interpret its communicative purpose. It enables a person not only to write and transcribe words but also to put them together in sentences (and compositions) in various ways to convey varied meanings to different audiences and for a range of purposes. The focus on sentence-level information not only has an impact on writing but also on reading comprehension and academic literacy overall (Lynch et al., 2021). When the sentence-level focus is delivered in tandem with content and analytical thinking, as it is in Combinations, students stand to benefit in more ways than one. The focus may be small (i.e., the sentence), but it is not simple. Combinations focuses students' attention on how language and meaning are interconnected. The strategies are sophisticated, meaning-driven (not code-based or basic) and high-yield; they advance analytical thinking and linguistic expression while asking students to think deeply about content and build knowledge simultaneously. These multiplier strategies support students who are learning English to develop what they need for academic literacy and empower teachers of multilingual learners to address seemingly insurmountable challenges.

Note

1 Currently, professional development in sentence strategies as a foundation for expository writing is available in three ways and from three different organizations: (1) *Writing is Thinking* (WIT, or WITsi when combined with SI) through Strategic Inquiry, https://strategicinquiry.com/workshops/ (2) *Advancing Thinking through Writing* through The Writing Revolution, https://www.thewritingrevolution.org/courses/ and (3) *Expository Writing* or "EXPO" (formerly Teaching Basic Writing Skills) through The Windward Institute, https://www.thewindwardschool.org/the-windward-institute.

References

Bunch, G. C., Kibler, A., & Pimentel, S. (2012). Realizing opportunities for English learners in the common core English language arts and disciplinary literacy standards. *Commissioned Papers on Language and Literacy Issues in the Common Core State Standards and Next Generation Science Standards*, 94(1), 1–16.

Escamilla, K., Olsen, L., & Slavick, J. (2022). *Towards comprehensive effective literacy policy and instruction for emergent bilingual/English learner students* [White paper]. National Committee for Effective Literacy. https://multilingualliteracy.org/wp-content/uploads/2022/04/21018-NCEL-Effective-Literacy-White-Paper-FINAL_v2.0.pdf

Gillis, M. B., & Eberhardt, N. C. (2018). *Syntax knowledge to practice.* Literacy How Professional Learning Series.

Goldenberg, C. (2022, April 14). Phonics instruction is not enough for English learners, or anyone. but it's still foundational for all. *Core Learning.* https://www.corelearn.com/phonics-instruction-for-english-learners

Haynes, C. W., Smith, S. L. & Laud, L. (2019). Structured literacy approaches to teaching written expression. *Perspectives on Language and Literacy*, Summer 2019, pp. 22–29. International Dyslexia Association.

Hennessey, N. (2022, February 16). Seriously, syntax matters: Critical connections to comprehension [Webinar]. *Pivot Learning.* https://www.pivotlearning.org/resources/syntax-and-reading-comprehension-webinar/

Hochman, J. C., & Wexler, N. (2017). *The writing revolution: A guide to advancing thinking through writing in all subjects and grades.* Jossey-Bass.

Knapp, P., & Watkins, M. (2005). *Genre, text, grammar: Technologies for teaching and assessing writing.* University of New South Wales Press Ltd.

Lesaux, N. K., Galloway, E. P., & Marietta, S. H. (2016). *Teaching advanced literacy skills: A guide for leaders in linguistically diverse schools.* Guilford Publications.

Lynch, E. M. E., Duncan, T. S., & Deacon, S. H. (2021). Informing the science of reading: Students' awareness of sentence-level information is important for reading comprehension. *Reading Research Quarterly*, 56(S1), S221–S230.

Moschkovich, J. (2012). Mathematics, the common core, and language: Recommendations for mathematics instruction for ELs aligned with the common core. *Commissioned Papers on Language and Literacy Issues in the Common Core State Standards and Next Generation Science Standards*, 94, 17.

National Academies of Sciences, Engineering, and Medicine. (2017). *Promoting the educational success of children and youth learning English: Promising futures*. National Academies Press. https://doi.org/10.17226/24677

National Center for Education Statistics. (2022, May). *English learners in public school*. Conditions of Education. U.S. Department of Education, Institute of Education Sciences. https://nces.ed.gov/programs/coe/indicator/cgf

New York State diploma requirements applicable to all students enrolled in grades 9-12. (2022, June). New York State Education Department. http://www.nysed.gov/common/nysed/files/currentdiplomarequirements.pdf

Olsen, L. (2010). *Reparable harm fulfilling the unkept promise of educational opportunity for California's long term English learners*. A Californians Together Research & Policy Publication. https://web.stanford.edu/~hakuta/Courses/Ed330X%20Website/Olsen_ReparableHarm2ndedition.pdf

Quinn, H., Lee, O., & Valdés, G. (2012). Language demands and opportunities in relation to next generation science standards for English language learners: What teachers need to know. *Commissioned Papers on Language and Literacy Issues in the Common Core State Standards and Next Generation Science Standards*, 94(2012), 32–32.

Scarborough, H. S. (2001). Connecting early language and literacy to later reading (dis)abilities: Evidence, theory, and practice. In S. Neuman & D. Dickinson (Eds.), *Handbook for research in early literacy* (pp. 97–110). Guilford Press.

Scott, C. M. (2009). A case for the sentence in reading comprehension. *Language, Speech, and Hearing Services in Schools*, 40(2), 184–191. https://doi.org/10.1044/0161-1461(2008/08-0042)

Sedita, J. (2019, December 1). The strands that are woven into skilled writing. *Keys to Literacy*. https://keystoliteracy.com/wp-content/uploads/2020/02/The-Strands-That-Are-Woven-Into-Skilled-WritingV2.pdf

Sedita, J. (2023) *The writing rope: A framework for explicit writing instruction in all subjects*. Paul H Brookes Publishing Co.

Shanahan, T. (2022, August 13). Trying again – What teachers need to know about sentence comprehension. *Shanahan On Literacy*. https://shanahanonliteracy.com/blog/trying-again-what-teachers-need-to-know-about-sentence-comprehension#sthash.Z9OHfmGY.dpbs

Spycher, P. (2007). Academic writing of adolescent English learners: Learning to use "although". *Journal of Second Language Writing*, *16*(4), 238–254. https://doi.org/10.1016/j.jslw.2007.07.001

Street, B. (2003). What's "new" in new literacy studies? Critical approaches to literacy in theory and practice. *Current Issues in Comparative Education*, *5*(2), 77–91.

Van Cleave, W. (2012). *Writing matters: Developing sentence skills in students of all ages – teachers manual*. V.C. Educational Consulting.

Wexler, N. (2022, September 23). To help students read and write, shower some love on the sentence. *Forbes*. https://www.forbes.com/sites/nataliewexler/2022/09/23/to-help-students-read-and-write-shower-some-love-on-the-sentence/?sh=6c9039385dbb

3

Combinations + Strategic Inquiry

Closing the Research–Implementation Gap for Multilingual Learners

Research makes clear that becoming a skilled and effective professional in serving culturally and linguistically diverse students requires substantive development in multiple domains, including: (1) knowledge of instructional design and pedagogy that integrates language with content; (2) enactment of effective and efficient instructional practices, including scaffolding and assessments; (3) asset-based beliefs about students and their potential and (4) motivation for developing pedagogical expertise (Walqui, 2007). Development across these domains is complex: involving knowledge about theory and research in language development; a large set of pedagogical strategies that must be practiced, honed and applied flexibly in varied contexts and adaptive elements involving the identities, cultural values, perceptions and experiences of the teachers themselves. Therefore, the mechanisms required to effectively develop teacher expertise in all domains need to be equally dynamic and responsive.

In theory, Combinations develops teachers in each of these domains. In practice, however, because the strategies are so different from what is typical, especially for middle and high school teachers for whom the length of written assignments is often associated with rigor, professional development in Combinations alone is insufficient for these strategies to fully take hold. We argue, however, that Combinations can fulfill its promise when utilized as the focus of adult learning within a structured design for teacher collaboration called Strategic Inquiry (SI) – a school reform model designed to anticipate and overturn cultural constraints to new learning and to change.

SI is a method of embedded, ongoing professional development in which teachers are empowered to identify and address areas of need for students who are outside the sphere of success and to lead to systemic improvements such that these students and others like them will become successful. It is a method of developing distributed leadership for shifting teacher thinking and practice – as well as schoolwide systems – in response to teacher-generated evidence of what struggling students need most. Through a structured process of teacher collaboration that links the micro and the macro (that enables teachers to understand how larger conditions and systems function to constrain some students' success, and how precisely they can be changed to enhance learning for those students), continuous improvement takes hold.

For a deep dive into SI, including its theory, evolution, impact and processes, we refer readers to *Strategic Inquiry: Starting Small for Big Results in Education* (Panero & Talbert, 2013). Our argument in this book is that the pairing of Combinations with SI is especially powerful for meeting the complex needs of teachers' professional learning to effectively support multilingual learners' success. So how does Combinations plus SI become greater than the sum of its parts, achieving more together through synergy than either can accomplish on its own?

To answer this question, we will first explain how Combinations alone can potentially advance each domain of teacher development. First, because each activity is embedded within content learning with an explicit focus on language and academic literacy, Combinations shows teachers concretely *how* language, literacy and content can be seamlessly and easily integrated in instruction. Second, because each small strategy provides immediate feedback regarding students' knowledge of both the language forms and the content assessed, it improves both instructional planning and practice. Since a teacher has to become extremely precise about the driving instructional objectives for both content and skill in order to design a Combinations activity, teachers who use Combinations learn to develop clarity and specificity in their teaching points. Combinations also cultivates the beliefs and mindsets needed to serve culturally and linguistically diverse students well. Simply put, teachers' self-efficacy improves when they see (a) students become immediately engaged as their precise learning needs are met; (b) students' writing, reading comprehension and oral expression rapidly improve as a result of intentional teaching of language with content and (c) tangible evidence of students' strengths – what they know and can do that is not always obvious. These in turn increase both student and teacher motivation for continued learning and improvement.

Despite the potential of Combinations in these domains, however, a teacher who can stay the course in implementing Combinations in their classroom after learning about Combinations through traditional professional development is rare. Individual teachers who come to professional development sessions often see the potential of the strategies to improve learning for students and implement them in their classroom immediately. Yet they are frequently frustrated or foiled in their attempts to use them consistently for a variety of reasons. First, the strategies entail a large amount of new learning. Teachers need ongoing support and feedback to hone their craft and to internalize how to design tasks that target and assess the most important content and language objectives. Second, teachers often receive pushback or even rebuke from administrators who lack training in language instruction and may believe (mistakenly) that Combinations is overly simple or basic. These administrators wonder whether sentence-level activities are rigorous, mistaking length for rigor rather than the level of language and content sophistication required for a task. In this sense, the strategies are counter-cultural. Third, the strategies will inevitably need to be adjusted and modified based on particular students' needs based on evidence. Without structured and protected collaborative time for teachers to talk with one another about particular students' needs and how to meet them, and without a chance to see that this time pays off in improved student performance and is thus worthwhile, Combinations is unlikely to take long-term hold in an individual teacher's classroom, let alone schoolwide. However, we show in this chapter what is often the case with instructional practices: retention significantly increases when teachers implement new strategies in the context of supported, structured and collaborative adult development (Knight, 2017).

SI as a model for school reform through investment in teacher teams has gone a long way in demonstrating impact generally, but our experiences and research suggest that it is far more powerful when paired with Combinations. SI has been found to shift teachers' focus from teaching (delivering what they already know) to learning (identifying learning gaps and how to meet them). This critical shift is necessary to advance teacher knowledge in the domains of pedagogical knowledge and instructional practices, since teachers cannot implement something they don't see as needed or haven't deeply learned to do. SI has also been found to develop teachers' shared accountability for students who are outside of the sphere of success and formative assessment practices that improve these and other students' learning (Talbert, et al., 2012; Wohlstetter et al., 2018). In a word, SI has been found to overcome the major shortcomings of more generic (less structured) forms of inquiry and professional development: failure to move teachers beyond the "culture of nice" (Horn & Little, 2010; MacDonald, 2011) and to demonstrably move the needle for student performance, especially for multilingual learners.

Key to the success of SI's design for inquiry, according to two iterations of independent research (Talbert et al., 2012; Wohlstetter et al., 2018), is a structured process for supporting teachers to drill down to identify precise areas of need for small groups of focal students, small enough to identify what exactly needs to be taught the next day. This key principle of "getting small", as it is referred to in the literature, allows for the movement and success of students who were not successful previously and has been found to shift teacher beliefs and mindsets rapidly and consistently. By "getting small", teachers see concretely and specifically the skills that still must be taught. When they see the impact of their targeted interventions in moving students' learning forward, their beliefs about the students' ability to learn and their own ability to improve the performance of these students are transformed (Panero & Talbert, 2013; Talbert et al., 2012). Success cultivates motivation among teachers to keep learning and to spread the work with colleagues; it has a spill-over effect in terms of improving instructional practices broadly by inculcating the teachers' new habit of seeking actionable evidence with which to challenge their own assumptions. Without training or the collaborative support of peers, teachers of multilingual learners often feel helpless, demoralized and disappointed, and lack confidence in their own ability to meet the needs of their students. With supported SI, a culture of learning that uplifts multilingual learners and all students takes hold.

It takes time for such transformation to take hold in a whole school. Our experience and research have led us to believe that the best way to accelerate student improvement and teacher buy-in through SI is to put Combinations at the center of teachers' collaborative work. In a typical SI process without Combinations, it takes teacher teams a long time – perhaps a full year – to identify where precisely students are getting stuck in their learning or to diagnose the root of the problem in pedagogy and instruction. This is because team members are carving this information out of stone; without close attention to academic literacy and strategic tools to focus this attention, there are many dead ends. In the highest performing school in the first large-scale iteration of SI when implemented as a strategy for large high school transformation in NYC (see Talbert et al., 2012), it took three full years before teams had enough confidence in what had been identified in terms of learning gaps and effective solutions to move forward with a systemic schoolwide response (See Tyre, 2012 for a description of the journey of this highly successful school).

However, after this first iteration of large-scale implementation of SI, we began to see patterns in learning gaps identified by over 100 inquiry teams as well as in effective strategies to meet those gaps. We began to wonder if teams new to the inquiry process could benefit from the learning of prior teams, standing on the shoulders of those who had come before. We began using a set of diagnostic tools that led teachers directly to using Combinations as a starting point for inquiry (see, for example, the sentence tracker and staircase described in Chapter 7). In the second large-scale implementation of SI with struggling high schools, we found that implementing Combinations up front and from the start led teams and schools to outsized and accelerated improvement. The granular sentence-level strategies quickly surfaced learning needs and effective ways to address them. High school teachers rapidly saw the need to address foundational academic literacy skills even if they had not previously felt that doing so was part of their job description. Arming teachers with effective ways to do so amplified rather than worked against content learning and cultivated buy-in quickly. As a result, the second independent evaluation of SI in struggling "Renewal" high schools in NYC found stronger outcomes in a much shorter time frame, despite fewer resources and support in a scaled train-the-facilitator model[1] (Wohlstetter et al., 2018).

The power of Combinations plus SI lies in the fact that the professional learning space created focuses teachers' collective attention on the fundamental skills needed for academic literacy and develops teachers' collective efficacy in transforming their own practice to meet these needs. By deeply studying the impact of Combinations, and, thereby, the impact of teaching academic literacy, teachers are able to tackle the root cause of why many students, including those identified as English learners, in particular, may be struggling academically overall. The strategies themselves make the needed granular elements of academic literacy visible and provide a concrete way to develop them in concert with content knowledge. The SI process makes possible the actual learning of what students need and what the strategies have to offer. At its core, SI develops powerful formative assessment practices; in order to pinpoint the precise learning that is needed, participants need to design more precise and granular assessments than those typically available in the teaching profession. Combinations tasks themselves function as excellent granular assessments. Having strategic language and content-based assessment tools at the center of teachers' professional learning provides a powerful model of how to get small and quickly capture teachers' attention; gives clear guidance about how to respond to what they are learning and simultaneously accelerates students' academic literacy. This primes the pump for expanding continuous learning. When teams wish to tackle other challenges in student learning for and beyond multilingual learners, they can draw upon a powerful model of how to get small to unlock and address these challenges.

Overall, SI plus Combinations fills significant gaps in current professional learning systems by addressing multiple domains of teacher expertise needed to serve linguistically diverse students. We summarize these ideas in Table 3.1.

So, what does SI plus Combinations look like in practice? How do the two together work on an actual team to get needed pedagogical knowledge and instructional practices into teacher practice and into the drinking water of a school? How do they work together to improve students' academic literacy while simultaneously developing asset-based beliefs and increased

Table 3.1 How SI + Combinations develops expertise for teaching multilingual learners across multiple domains

Domain	SI + Combinations…
Knowledge of instructional design and pedagogy	Makes academic literacy skills clear and discrete. Accelerates understanding of the need for language and content-integrated curriculum and instruction to develop academic literacy for multilingual learners.
Instructional practices	Makes instructional practices for closing academic literacy gaps explicit and clear. Makes it clear how to teach language and content together. Delivers immediate feedback so teachers can be responsive and shift practice quickly.
Mindsets and beliefs	Provides evidence of what multilingual learners are able to do in clear and actionable ways so that teachers' beliefs about what students can do and what teachers are capable of quickly change.
Motivation	Creates space for social and collaborative support along with the resources teachers need to feel successful and willing to continue refining their practice in light of what often feel like significant challenges.
Reflection	Supports teachers to reflect and make evidence-based decisions in timely and intentional ways alongside colleagues so that the context of development is not just individual but also collective. The process of reflection in SI brings together the teachers' action and learning in all the other domains of teacher expertise.

motivation for teachers and develop a learning culture in a school? The following scenario, a composite created based on real experiences we have led and witnessed as part of our work with New York City high schools, illustrates how these ambitious goals are developed.

> Gotham High is a large urban high school made up of a student population where 22% of students are designated as English learners. These students have been perpetual victims of a system not designed for them, moving from class to class and year to year without yet reaching English language proficiency as determined by the state. Many were born in the US and use English as their primary language. Many also have not been supported by their school system to develop academic literacy and have experienced struggles with reading comprehension and poor performance on state exams as a result.
>
> The principal of Gotham High School, Felicia Rodriguez, wanted to get to the bottom of why these students were getting stuck. A read-through of their essays made it clear to her that the students had not been getting the support they needed to meet the demands of the academic writing tasks required of them. The students were mostly on the right track with the content, it seemed, but their writing was unelaborated and lacked detail. When Ms. Rodriguez talked to these students to learn about their experiences, she was struck by how many of them just seemed to hate writing.
>
> Looking for a way to focus intentionally on the needs of these students, Ms. Rodriguez brought together teacher teams for SI. She created one inquiry team per grade level, asking each team to focus on students the teachers taught in common with an emphasis on analysis and improvement of student writing. Ms. Rodriguez knew that previous inquiry teams at other schools had identified patterns in students' learning needs and sentence-level strategies that were effective in addressing them. So, Ms. Rodriguez's teams started with tools that would help target areas in literacy where her

focal students were likely to need substantial support. Ms. Rodriguez also sent her teams to professional development workshops to learn about Combinations. Equipped with Combinations as a set of instructional routines and with protected time for inquiry, Ms. Rodriguez set her teacher teams up to get to the bottom of what would help their students who were deemed to be long-term English learners.

The ninth-grade team began by gathering a baseline expository paragraph from students in response to a simple prompt: to describe someone who was a hero to them and why. They then analyzed this baseline writing sample with the "Where do I begin" tool (see Appendix A). The purpose of this tool is to gather evidence to help teacher teams determine what they should focus upon first: sentence or paragraph skills. At first glance at student work, teachers often select paragraph skills to address first. The SI process, given its focus on getting small and gathering evidence from student work, helped this team arrive at a different conclusion. In previous iterations of SI, teachers had learned over time that teams often gravitated to paragraph skills because they themselves did not know of specific ways to help students to improve (rather than to correct) their sentences. If their students' sentences were grammatically correct, teachers didn't necessarily see that there was anything more to be done, that in fact they might be missing an opportunity to help students to improve these sentences. With the "Where do I begin" tool, the team was surprised to find that according to the tool, the students needed or at least could benefit from sentence-level interventions even more than with paragraph ones.

To get smaller, the team then used a second tool called a "sentence tracker" (See Appendix B). This SI tool helps teachers identify a more specific area of focus within sentences. Team members noticed right away that the tools they were using allowed them to look at specific students and their specific needs very rapidly. "This is really different from how we did inquiry in my last school", math teacher Lydia Pomona said.

> There we looked at data too, but we spent a lot of time with larger data sets and aggregate data. Getting really quickly into looking at our students' writing with a tool that helps us know what exactly to look for feels really meaningful, and different.

By looking at the evidence, the team came to see what their principal had noticed: that the sentences of their focal students were mostly correct, but that they were simple, unelaborated and lacked detail. In looking more closely (following the guidance provided by the sentence tracker), they noticed that very few students had used any of the three conjunctions "but", "because" or "so". Two teachers stated that the students might know these conjunctions, but did not use them on this task. "They're in ninth-grade after all; how could they not know them?" social studies teacher Gerard Greene said. But he and others had to admit that they really didn't know for sure. They agreed to focus on these conjunctions as their first area of study as a team, reasoning that knowing them would help students write more complex sentences and support content learning across their different subject areas.

The Because, But & So strategy (BBS, see Chapter 4 for further explanation) is designed to support students to add complexity in their expression of content-based meaning. A teacher designs one stem that can be completed with all three conjunctions, ensuring not only that students must learn and apply the meaning (precise function) of each conjunction but also that they have to think deeply about many aspects of the content. **Because** pulls for a reason, **but** pulls for an exception and **so** pulls for cause and effect. At a Combinations workshop, the teachers were shown how to design BBS activities to pull for essential content. The team collaborated to review what they had learned and to design BBS activities that each would teach the following week. They agreed to bring back the resulting student work for review.

In the next series of meetings, again by drawing on tools developed previously and with the help of an SI facilitator, the team became increasingly precise in identifying what their students knew and did not know in terms of BBS and their content. At one meeting, they zoomed in to study one student (Kareem, a pseudonym), whom three of the teachers taught, to further their discovery process. At this meeting, the team's charge was to identify what Kareem knew and did not know according to the evidence provided for both content (as demonstrated in each task) and the BBS skill (as demonstrated across tasks). A tracker was designed to support the team in this task. It had space for each teacher to identify whether the evidence suggested that Kareem had mastered the content called for in their particular task. What would be aggregated (counted) across teachers was evidence of whether or not Kareem truly understood and could utilize the conjunctions "because", "but" and "so" properly; the team was charged with coming to a collective decision in response to this question.

To meet their charge, team members read Kareem's work products closely and completed the tracker based upon the evidence. In looking at Kareem's work, team members initially said that, according to the evidence, Kareem had not yet mastered "because, but & so", although they agreed he seemed to have a strong grasp of content. The living environment teacher, Nina Reilly, pointed to Kareem's written responses on the task for her class (see Figure 3.1). "It's filled with run-ons", she said. "He knows the science, but I don't think he understands how to use BBS". Two other teachers nodded. Then the English teacher, Marco James, spoke up. "Wait", he said. "I see he's writing run-ons. But the conjunctions are used correctly. He knows what they mean. And look what he wrote in economics. He didn't

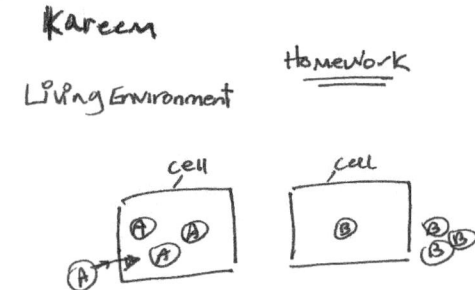

FIGURE 3.1 Kareem's writing sample – BBS in living environment.

write run-ons there. I wonder what's going on there" (see Figure 3.2). There was a pause in conversation. Then the living environment teacher, Ms. Reilly, spoke again: "Maybe my task was too open", she said. "I just told the students to write about passive and active transport using BBS. It wasn't as structured as the other tasks". "Remember how at the Combinations workshops they kept saying that the format of the tasks really matters?" Mr. James chimed in.

> That we needed to write the stems for the students, and to try out the answers first to make sure it worked. They even wanted us to format the task in a certain way – kind of how you did it, Mr. Greene – to really show that we wanted one single sentence from the students. I think the way you did it, Mr. Greene, really helped Kareem.

A histogram is a helpful statistical graph because __it shows the largest and the smallest frequence.__

A histogram is a helpful statistical graph, but __you have to create a table before the graph.__

A histogram is a helpful historical graph, so __you can see it visually.__

FIGURE 3.2 Kareem's writing sample – BBS in economics

"Thanks", said Mr. Greene.

> But actually, I'm not really sure Kareem has a totally solid understanding of 'so' as indicating cause and effect. Look at the third sentence in mine (see Figure 3.3): 'Industrialization was important for the US… so employees suffer.' I don't think he's using "so" the right way there. I can't really tell that for sure if he understands how to use it.

"He didn't use "so" at all in my activity", Ms. Reilly said. "I didn't realize that until now. He seemed to get it in the economics task, but I really think we need more evidence".

1. Industrialization was important for the United States in the late 1800s because __People needed coal by mines.__

2. Industrialization was important for the United States in the late 1800s, but __it harms people and children to mine.__

3. Industrialization was important for the United States in the late 1800s, so __employees suffer from illness, disease and mining.__

FIGURE 3.3 Kareem's writing sample – BBS in social studies.

> By the end of the inquiry session, the team decided that although Kareem's content knowledge seemed strong, they needed better information to determine what precisely Kareem did and did not know in terms of the studied conjunctions. Ms. Reilly was clear about how she was going to adjust her task for the following lesson (by crafting the sentence stems carefully, doing the anticipated responses ahead of time and formatting the activity as the economics and social studies teachers had done); she was clear that doing so would allow her to see more clearly what Kareem was truly able to do. The teachers also agreed that reinforcement with "so" was required – they wanted to make sure Kareem truly understood the meaning of "so" and could fluently produce sentences demonstrating cause and effect. They agreed that they would each implement an additional BBS task, being sure that their activity included the conjunction "so", and would bring Kareem's resulting student work to their next inquiry meeting. They were excited to see the result of their interventions at their next meeting.

This story reflects the experiences of numerous teams and teachers we have worked with who have implemented the same strategies, used the same tools and had similar conversations. While every school is different and every team is on its own journey, a few outcomes are reliably consistent, namely that Combinations helps teachers to do what they once thought was impossible. It helps them see academic literacy needs that were previously invisible, and it helps them understand in a concrete and practical way that there are particular literacy skills without which students cannot express their academic knowledge. In the context of collaborative inquiry, where the tools used to guide teacher conversations and analysis are as granular as the Combinations strategies themselves are for students, the inquiry process allows teachers to see what in their own practice needs to change and why. Focusing first on student work, rather than directly at first on teacher practice, allows teachers to come to see the limitations in their practice more organically and less defensively, because they immediately see the impact of their instructional decisions on student performance. The initial focus on student work, use of granular tools and requirement to use evidence create a trusting environment in which it becomes safe for teachers to link cause and effect (teacher practice to student work) themselves. It is this experiential (gut-level) awareness of the direct link between changes in teacher practice and the resulting change in student performance that truly changes teachers and teaching culture (Gallimore et al., 2009).

Combinations provides an effective and efficient way to develop many of the challenging tasks that teachers need to accelerate learning for multilingual learners. When used with a proven and structured form of collaborative inquiry, teachers' beliefs about their students and their own capacities are supercharged. It is this pairing of Combinations plus SI that we truly believe is a game changer for multilingual learners' success.

Note

1 Between 2014 and 2016, Combinations plus SI was implemented as the core instructional improvement strategy for all 35 of New York City's most struggling "renewal" high schools. Unlike the first iteration of SI for struggling high schools in NYC (Talbert et al., 2012), where external SI facilitators were deployed full time to support participating schools, this second iteration of SI used a much less resource-intensive train-the-facilitator approach where SI/Combinations consultants trained school-based teacher leaders as internal SI/Combinations facilitators inside each school. These school-based facilitators were developed in real time, learning the work at professional development sessions as they simultaneously led the work with their school teams and exponentially growing on-site leaders as they gradually developed their own colleagues over the two years. Findings from the evaluation found that results were even stronger for student improvement and the development of school capacity than in the first iteration (Talbert et al., 2012; Wohlstetter et al., 2018).

References

Horn, I. S., & Little, J. W. (2010). Attending to problems of practice: Routines and resources for professional learning in teachers' workplace interactions. *American Educational Research Journal, 47*(1), 181–217.

Gallimore, R., Ermeling, B. A., Saunders, W. M., & Goldenberg, C. (2009). Moving the learning of teaching closer to practice: Teacher education implications of school-based inquiry teams. *The Elementary School Journal, 109*(5), 537–553.

Knight, J. (2017). *The impact cycle: What instructional coaches should do to foster powerful improvements in teaching.* Corwin Press.

MacDonald, E. (2011). When nice won't suffice: Honest discourse is key to shifting school culture. *Journal of Staff Development, 32*(3), 45–47, 51.

Panero, N. S., & Talbert, J. E. (2013). *Strategic inquiry: Starting small for big results in education.* Harvard Education Press.

Talbert, J. E., Cor, M. K., Chen, P. R., Kless, L. M., & McLaughlin, M. (2012). Inquiry-based school reform: Lessons from SAM in NYC. *Center for Research on the Context of Teaching at Stanford University [Program Evaluation].* http://www.academia.edu/29864629/Inquiry-based_School_Reform_Lessons_from_SAM_in_NYC

Tyre, P. (2012). The writing revolution. *The Atlantic, 19.* https://www.theatlantic.com/magazine/archive/2012/10/the-writing-revolution/309090/

Walqui, A. (2007). The development of teacher expertise to work with adolescent English learners: A model and a few priorities. In L. S. Verplaetse & N. Migliacci (Eds.), *Inclusive pedagogy for English language learners: A handbook of research-informed practices* (pp. 103–125). Lawrence Erlbaum.

Wohlstetter, P., Kim, E., Flack, C. B., & Mat, A. (2018). Strategic inquiry and New York City's renewal high schools. *Teachers College Columbia University, November.* https://www.tc.columbia.edu/media/news/images/2018/december/Wohlstetter_Strategic-Inquiry-Final-Report-1.0-1.pdf

Part II
Getting into the Work

4
Sentence Boundaries

A critical foundation of academic literacy is knowledge of *sentence boundaries*. All students, including multilingual learners, must understand, on a basic level, at least what is and is not a sentence. This includes knowledge of where a sentence begins and ends; the elements that constitute it and how to apply punctuation and capitalization to enforce these boundaries and to delineate a discrete idea.

When students are learning English as a new language, unlocking the patterns of basic syntax and how words work together to form sentences provides parameters for how to make meaning. Tracking where a sentence begins and ends, and therefore tracking the set of propositions laid out from sentence to sentence, helps students to both build comprehension of a text when they read (Chen et al., 2018) as well as learn how to use language structures to communicate meaning in written expression (Shanahan, 2022; Wexler, 2022).

Many students across K-12 grade levels in US schools, including but in no way limited to multilingual learners, have not been taught these basic skills explicitly and/or effectively, and therefore move through the grades without being provided a solid understanding of sentence boundaries. This impedes their ability to communicate ideas clearly in writing and may also impede their reading comprehension (Hennessy, 2022; Snow, 2002). Over time, these students are asked to build more complex sentences (a key skill for academic literacy) on a shaky foundation, with a weak understanding of the skeletal underpinnings upon which more complex forms are built.

In this chapter, we present a set of strategies that can be quickly integrated across grades and subjects to teach sentence boundaries to multilingual learners (and all students) while also reinforcing academic content and thinking. Because they are small and manageable, include both receptive and productive options, can be easily differentiated and offer opportunities to draw flexibly upon their home language, these strategies make learning sentence basics in concert with meaning accessible for students learning English.

Two caveats: first, while the strategies we present in this chapter do support and reinforce content knowledge, the most heavy-hitting strategies in combinations for content are presented in the upcoming chapters. For this reason, teachers of some upper-grade subjects (such as mathematics) may choose *not* to teach sentence boundary strategies. Secondly, not all students need instruction in sentence boundaries. (The case study in Chapter 8 addresses the issue of how teachers determine which students need which strategies.) For teachers who want to start with the most heavy-hitting strategies for content and/or whose students already have a strong knowledge of sentence boundaries, we recommend beginning with Chapter 5.

What Is the Gap in Teaching English Sentence Boundaries to Multilingual Learners, and How Does Our Approach Fill It?

In general, teachers of multilingual learners lack concrete or meaningful ways to develop students' knowledge of sentence basics in concert with academic content. Teachers of multilingual learners often notice that their students need instruction to support communication – orally and in writing – when they have not yet developed the understanding of language structures in English that will allow them to express their ideas fully. They notice unintentional fragments that limit the full expression of students' ideas. They observe extensive run-ons without sufficient attention to how ideas are organized and linked to communicate their ideas clearly. While this may be developmentally natural for a certain period as students learn a new language, teachers often wrongly assume that students will learn English sentence boundaries on their own, not realizing the methods or benefits of direct instruction in sentence boundaries. Without such intervention, a significant number of these students continue to experience reading and writing struggles as they are asked to meet more demanding requirements in academic literacy (Rhinehart et al., 2022).

We have observed that teachers, not knowing what else to do, often respond to students' need for instruction in sentence boundaries by teaching grammar – by teaching parts of speech, definitions of subject and predicate, rules for punctuation, etc. While we are not saying that teachers should *never* teach grammar, it is important to note the ways in which traditional grammar instruction as the primary way to teach sentence basics is highly problematic. First, it is often ineffective, as decades of research provide robust evidence that teaching grammar in isolation does not improve writing quality (Anderson et al., 1985; Hillocks & Smith, 1991) and that it may even have a slight negative effect (Graham & Perin, 2007). Second, a de-contextualized approach to grammar and language is particularly ineffective for students who are learning English; after all, a subject and predicate aren't any different from one another for a student for whom English is an unfamiliar language. Third and perhaps most importantly, it is inefficient. Teaching grammar in isolation is time-consuming – taking time away from other tasks involving reading and writing development and content learning – as it is often challenging for students to understand an abstract grammatical concept such as a *predicate* separately from its function in authentic communication. Teachers of multilingual learners in particular have no time to waste in accelerating academic literacy; they must build knowledge of language and content simultaneously without sacrificing attention to meaning, audience or purpose.

Our approach fills the gap in existing practice by providing a menu of strategies that allow teachers to meet students where they are and build knowledge of sentence basics in concert with academic content and thinking. The strategies support students' ability to manipulate and extract meaning in sentences, a necessary component of academic literacy. When students understand the connection between how sentences work in relation to their meaning, they are able to read and write better. They can leverage their knowledge of syntax to support improved comprehension, build knowledge and support their learning and thinking overall.

While the strategies may seem simple on their face, what is challenging in our approach is designing the tasks so that they target precisely what students need for language learning and maximize their potential in developing that language knowledge along with essential academic content. Below, we introduce three buckets of strategies (each has a few variations), focusing on how each strategy (a) develops both sentence and content knowledge; (b) can be best designed and taught to ensure that it fulfills its promise in both domains and (c) functions as a granular formative assessment, letting the teacher know what precisely to teach next in both language and content.

Bucket One: Sorts, Parts & Scrambles

Multilingual learners, especially newcomers, often need more receptive tasks and a number of "at bats" to see and observe patterns in language before applying and using specific target language and skills. A scaffolded way of teaching and solidifying students' understanding of what is and is not a sentence – while also reinforcing academic content and thinking – is through the receptive tasks of sentence sorts, parts and scrambles, each of which increases in difficulty in terms of both language and content. These tasks require students to pay close attention to the order of words used to convey the intended idea and meaning in a sentence. Students need to closely read and use their understanding of the content in order to establish the conceptually accurate relationships between ideas expressed through word order in these tasks. In doing so, the tasks develop syntactic awareness in ways that are integrated with meaningful content.

In the *sentence sorts* activity (see Figure 4.1), the teacher provides a set of manipulatives, or sentence strips, that contain both sentences and fragments. Students are then asked to sort these sentence strips into one of two piles, depending on whether each

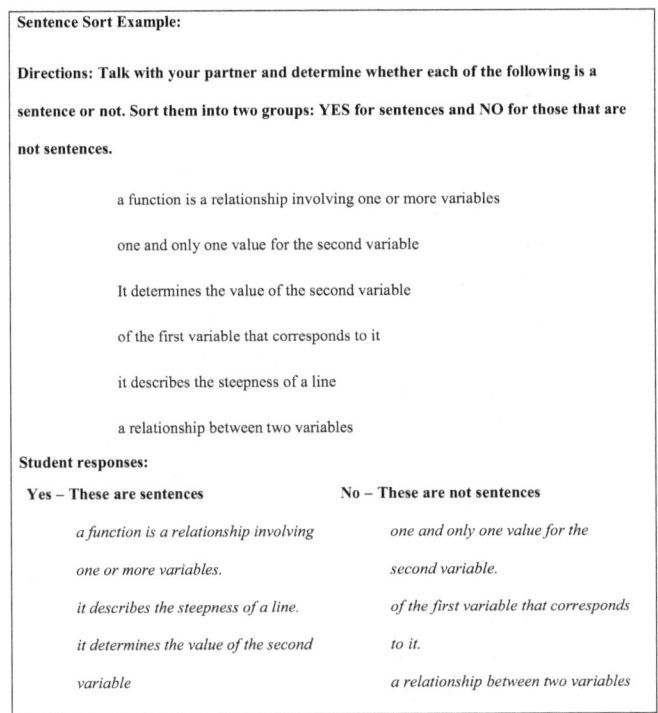

FIGURE 4.1 An example of sentence sorts strategy using content students might be learning.

strip is a sentence or a fragment. Note in these examples, directions are bolded and student responses are italicized.

In the *sentence parts* activity (see Figure 4.2), the teacher also provides manipulatives or sentence strips, but in this case each

Sentence Parts Example:

Directions: Match the parts to create three sentences about the charge of subatomic particles. Be sure to capitalize and punctuate your sentences.

has a negative charge	has a positive charge
has zero charge	the neutron
the proton	the electron

Student Responses:
The proton has a negative charge.
The neutron has a positive charge.
The electron has zero charge.

FIGURE 4.2 An example of sentence parts using content students might be learning.

strip includes one half of a sentence that the student must match with its other half in order for the sentence to make sense and be complete. This, like the sorts activity, is a receptive task, but it requires more intuition of sentence basics that students must apply than the prior activity. It also requires more knowledge of content, because matching parts correctly requires grammatical and content-based meaning and accuracy. A student could, for example, match parts in a way that is grammatically correct, but that represents a misconception regarding the content. This of course would provide important formative assessment information (feedback) to the teacher.

Finally, there is the *sentence scrambles* activity (see Figure 4.3), where the teacher also provides manipulatives or sentence strips. However, in this case, each strip contains just one piece of a grammatically correct sentence and students must unscramble all the provided parts to make a complete sentence that expresses accurate meaning about the content. This activity can range from simple to extremely complex for both language and content. We do not recommend using scrambles with students who are still learning to distinguish sentences from fragments. For most other students, the activity will solidify knowledge of sentence boundaries while powerfully reinforcing and assessing academic content.

Note that while these activities do not require students to produce language, by creating the strips using content students are studying, the teacher reinforces academic vocabulary and content in connection with teaching basic sentences. This also

---

Sentence Scramble Example:

Directions: Put the scrambled words in the right order to make a sentence. Capitalize and punctuate your sentence.

increases the rate also temperature as the reaction increases of

Student response:

As the temperature increases, the rate of reaction also increases.

FIGURE 4.3 An example of sentence scramble using content students might be learning.

makes the sentence forms clearer (since function is directly connected to meaning) than if these skills were taught through a traditional grammar exercise.

There are three things to note at this point about these and all Combinations strategies. First, when a teacher first introduces any Combinations strategy, they should do so with known vocabulary and content; this reduces the cognitive load required for students to learn how the new strategy actually works. In all other cases, however, these strategies should be designed using (and thus reinforcing) essential academic vocabulary and content.

Second, the strategies should be designed to allow access to this essential vocabulary and content regardless of a student's level of English language proficiency. This activity can and should be differentiated according to the student's specific sentence-level and language needs. For students with little exposure to formal education or lower levels of home language literacy, for example, the sentence structure in the sorts and parts activities should be very simple – with capitalization and punctuation provided, because the student probably needs these clues (in the sorts activity); and with the student asked to link a simple subject with a simple predicate (in the parts activity). With sorts, parts and scrambles, the teacher is always making strategic decisions about what to include and in what manner (whether or not to include the punctuation inside or outside of the sentence strips, for example) depending upon the students' knowledge of sentence basics.

Third, the teaching of these strategies, like all strategies in Combinations, allows teachers to integrate many best practices in quality instruction for multilingual learners, including providing opportunities for students to talk with one another and draw on their home language in instruction. For example, in a lesson utilizing sorts, parts and scrambles, students can discuss what they see in the sentences and fragments (in English and/or home language) as they physically sort the strips. This kind of instruction provides a real-time formative assessment opportunity as teachers ask students to verbalize their thinking and how they arrived at their decisions. The key is to surface and correct misconceptions and to prompt students' metalinguistic awareness about the language they are sorting. (See Vignette B for an illustration of these practices in action.)

Bucket Two: Identifying and Repairing Fragments

This bucket of activities is both receptive and productive in that it requires students to distinguish sentences from fragments *and* to repair identified fragments by supplying missing information based on the content that is being studied. Like the strategies in bucket one, the challenge here is designing each task so that it targets students' precise sentence-building needs *while* pulling for (reinforcing and assessing) essential content and thinking. When carefully designed to do both, these small strategies take little instructional time yet deliver big results.

First, students learn to *identify and repair fragments*. In this strategy, the teacher provides a short list of sentences and fragments using academic content that students are learning. Students distinguish the sentences from the fragments (a receptive task) and then repair the identified fragments (a productive task). To do so, they must supply the missing information (drawing upon and reinforcing academic content), use English syntax and vocabulary and capitalize and punctuate the sentences as appropriate for the meaning (see Figure 4.4). Note that in designing the task, teachers do not capitalize or punctuate the fragments or sentences, since doing so would give the answers away. Teachers do capitalize proper nouns because not doing so might be confusing to students.

Once students can identify and repair fragments when provided with a list, teachers can release some scaffolding by asking students to identify the ONE fragment that has been planted in a short (otherwise correct) paragraph, as in the two examples in Figure 4.5. For this activity, the teacher capitalizes and punctuates the fragment (the opposite of the case in Figure 4.4) so as not to give the answer away.

Again, the challenge in designing high-impact Combinations activities is two-fold. The first challenge is to target and provide practice in the precise language skill the students need most. (If the activity is designed to provide practice in a very specific

Directions: Write S if you see a sentence. Write F if you see a fragment. If S, rewrite it with capitalization and punctuation. If F, repair the fragment using information you have learned about the topic.

__S__ farm workers should be protected

__F__ the United Farm Workers hoped to

__S__ some believe the goals of labor unions are unrealistic

Student Responses:
Farm workers should be protected.
The United Farm Workers hoped to improve the job of workers.
Some believe the goals of labor unions are unrealistic.

FIGURE 4.4 Example of students identifying sentences and fragments.

language objective, then it will also provide the teacher with precise formative assessment information about what exactly to teach/assess next.) The second is to design the task for maximum benefit in terms of content.

In terms of the first challenge, consider the experiences of Lydia Adegbola, the English Department Chair at New Rochelle High School, who identified that some of her 12th graders were struggling with sentence boundaries. Although she thought only a few students needed direct instruction in this area, she decided to ask her whole class to identify and repair fragments in a list, thinking it would serve as a useful formative assessment. The results seemed to confirm her initial beliefs. After working on

Example 1:

Directions: Underline and then repair the one fragment in the following paragraph.

Have you ever seen a shark? Sharks are apex predators. They have rows of teeth. Sharks have gills. <u>They don't have</u>. They live alone. Sharks are interesting creatures.

Repaired Sentence:
<u>Sharks don't have bones.</u>

Example 2:

Directions: Underline and then repair the one fragment in the following paragraph.

After discovering that her father wants her to marry Paris, Juliet is distressed. First, she begs her mother not to force her to marry Paris. Her mother is steadfast. Next, she turns to her confidante, the nurse. <u>Confides in her and asks for a way to avoid this marriage</u>. The nurse also encourages Juliet to marry Paris. Juliet feels betrayed by the adults in her life.

Repaired sentence:
<u>Juliet confides in her and asks for a way to avoid this marriage.</u>

FIGURE 4.5 Examples of student responses to identify the fragment in a paragraph when the teacher capitalizes and punctuates the fragment.

sorts and parts with just a few students she believed needed this support, she then moved on to the next task: asking her whole class to identify and repair the one fragment in an otherwise correct paragraph. This time, Lydia was surprised to see that 15 out of 22 students in the class were not able to identify and repair the fragment correctly. When she looked more closely at her two tasks/assessments, she began to understand why. Her first task/assessment (identifying and repairing fragments in a list) included fragments that were either subjects or predicates and where the fragments were shorter than any of the sentences that she provided (see example 1 in Figure 4.5 as an example). Her second task/assessment, however, included ONE fragment that was quite long – long enough that many students assumed it must be a sentence (see example 2 in Figure 4.5). What this activity/assessment uncovered for Lydia was the reality that many of her students' knowledge of sentence boundaries in terms of function (rather than form) was not as solid as she had previously believed.

Lydia decided to test this new assumption by creating a new activity/assessment (identifying fragments/sentences in a list) that included a larger range of distractors (items that target potential misconceptions). This time, she included both short and long sentences and short and long fragments; fragments that contained just subjects or predicates and fragments that contained clauses. The results confirmed that the majority of students in Lydia's class did in fact need more instruction and practice to solidify their knowledge of sentence boundaries. They were 12th graders, so Lydia was relieved she had a way of teaching this needed knowledge along with (not separate from and in addition to) academic content, since they had no time to waste.

In terms of the second challenge (designing for maximum content learning), consider how a small change in task design can make a big difference in the quality of the task both to reinforce content knowledge and to assess it. See Figure 4.6 as an example.

One challenge in Combinations task design is being clear about what information the task requires the students themselves

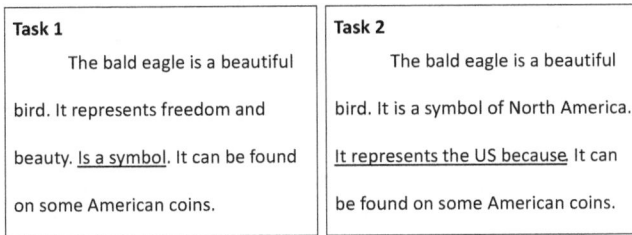

FIGURE 4.6 Example task designs for students to repair a sentence fragment.

to provide versus what information is actually provided by the task. In task one, students can correctly repair the fragment by providing only the term "the bald eagle". They are not called upon to articulate their knowledge of what the bald eagle represents, since that information is already provided in the task. Task one, therefore, does not function as a quality formative assessment for the objective, because it does not truly provide the information the teacher needs in order to know whether the students have met this objective. It tells the teacher only that students know that the bald eagle is a symbol, but not that they can independently explain what the eagle is a symbol of.

With slight modifications in task design, however, task two now functions as a quality formative assessment for the content objective. The selection and design of the fragment now emphasize different information – the *reason* that the bald eagle represents the US as a symbol – and require students to supply this reason. The task (in terms of what it requires students to do and how it functions as an assessment) and the objective are now aligned.

Designing quality Combinations tasks – those that leverage sentence and content learning simultaneously – is harder than it might look. It takes time and usually more than one set of eyes to get this right. We argue that their potential to do so much so efficiently makes it well worth the time spent. When you get them right, students' academic language, content learning, analytical thinking and expressive and reading comprehension abilities explode.

Bucket Three: Sentence Types

Once students have a basic command of sentence boundaries, we recommend teaching sentence types. For this activity, a teacher chooses important content that requires analysis and asks students to write four different sentences about the same topic: a statement, a question, an exclamation and a command as seen in Figure 4.7.

This activity requires students to use language in a variety of different ways to think and to write about the same content. It provides practice in a range of English language structures, because the construction of different sentence types necessitates changes in syntax. As with all Combinations activities, teachers should use their home language to support students' language and content learning. Teachers can ask students to write the four sentences in English and then translate the sentences back into their home language, or the other way around. This may be a needed scaffold to help them complete the task. In doing so,

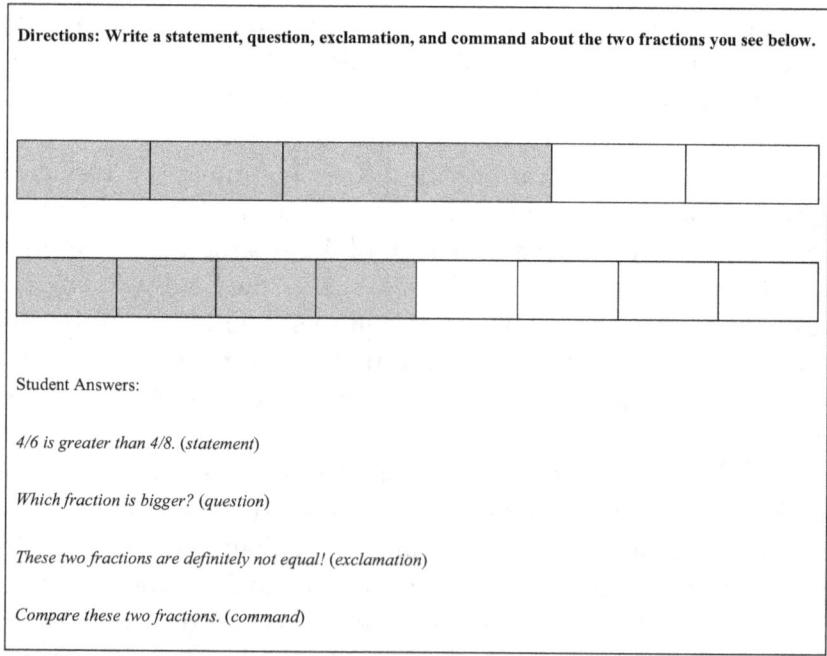

FIGURE 4.7 Example of student responses writing a statement, a question, an exclamation and a command on the same topic.

> **Directions: Write a question for each given answer.**
>
> **Q:** What is released when an electron loses energy?
> **A:** *electromagnetic radiationin the formof light*
>
> **Q:** What are reactions called that absorb heat?
> **A:** *endothermic*
>
> **Q:** When do molecules produce effective collisions?
> **A:** *when they have proper orientation + enoughenergy*

FIGURE 4.8 Example of student writing questions and answering them.

they may also generate new insights about the content they are learning.

Variations on this activity include that students can write their own questions about topics they are studying to which they or their classmates then provide the answers. They can also be asked to provide a question for a given answer, as in the science example in Figure 4.8. This is a rigorous activity for language and content, and it becomes increasingly rigorous for content when students are asked to provide not just a question for which multiple answers will suffice, but instead a question for which the provided answer is the *only* correct answer.

Design and Implementation Tips and Considerations for Sentence Boundaries

First, be kind to yourself and take your time. These strategies (like all those in Combinations) are harder to create than they look. It takes time to design a top-notch strategy – one that targets (and thus provides quality formative assessment information) for both language and content objectives simultaneously. We strongly recommend that you work with at least one other colleague when you design tasks; it's so helpful to have more than one pair of eyes and someone to talk through ideas. We also suggest that as you design, you ALWAYS imagine you are sitting in the seat of one or two particular students and you actually write out the anticipated student responses to each task – what you imagine students would actually write. This provides invaluable feedback on your task and how you might need to revise it. If you end up giving a task that does not elicit what you had hoped, do not despair! Every task provides formative assessment information not just about what the students know and need next, but also about your task design itself. You can always tweak your task for the next time.

Second, remember that the tasks as presented here in our examples can and must be adjusted in response to ongoing evidence of your particular students' needs. Success with Combinations requires you to constantly seek and respond to evidence of how your students use language and think about the content. Students who are still developing knowledge of sentence boundaries, for example, will need activities comprising more basic sentence structures. With sorts and parts, for example, you might begin with only simple subjects and predicates to be matched, rather than including prepositional phrases at the start. If a student is unable to complete a particular task, a well-designed activity will provide information about why. A well-designed parts activity, in other words, will tell you both whether the student understands the function of a subject and predicate as they are communicating meaning about particular content AND whether they have a solid grasp of the content at hand. Often, a student cannot complete a task the way we want because the task itself has not been designed properly or clearly. Teachers of Combinations should be on the lookout for aspects of their own tasks that need to be adjusted. Do not feel bad about this, as creating strong tasks is difficult. Combinations entails a learning process for students and teachers alike! (See Vignette A for a teacher working with a colleague to design a strong sentence boundary task.)

Finally, *draw upon everything you know about effective instruction for multilingual learners, including the need to model, teach explicitly, support as much conversation as possible and develop metalinguistic awareness.* Activities should always draw on essential vocabulary and content. Start small and be explicit. Draw on student's home language assets, knowing that students may need to annotate key vocabulary in their home language for words they do not yet automatically recognize. Invite students to read aloud and talk with each other about the tasks as much as possible. Specifically, teachers should provide opportunities for students to:

- Compare how sentences and language structures work in English and in their home language, explicitly helping students create cross-linguistic connections and comparisons;
- Discuss with peers and verbally articulate their observations about how language works in the specific tasks they are working on;
- Discuss the logic of how they solved the problem in the task in connection to the content and meaning of the examples and
- Build metalinguistic awareness and how this connects to their use of home language. Students should be able to name and articulate their understanding of what constitutes a sentence; where a sentence begins and ends and why a given example is a sentence or a fragment.

These methods enable you to design activities that better assess your students' needs.

In Vignette A, we illustrate how teachers can work together to improve the quality of their task design. This vignette emphasizes how teachers need to clarify their objectives and look closely at whether the tasks they design are aligned to those objectives. It shows the need for anticipating student responses by imagining how multilingual learners might answer a task in order to ensure that the task design gets at the right language structures and content.

VIGNETTE A   Designing a strong task together

Ms. Tucker is a first-grade teacher and teaches with her ELD co-teacher, Mr. Chen. They are reading the story of the Three Little Pigs with their first graders and are meeting together during their prep period to design a Repairing Fragments task that would be used as an exit ticket for an upcoming lesson. The content objective for the lesson was for students to explain the character traits of the characters in the story. Now, they need to write the fragments that students will repair in a new complete sentence using their understanding of the story.

Ms. Tucker: I think this is straightforward. We can provide the beginning of the sentence, just the fragment. The kids can provide the rest.

She writes down "the wolf is" on a piece of scrap paper.

Mr. Chen: The anticipated response would be [writing as he speaks] *The wolf is deceitful.* Or students might just write, *The wolf is bad.* That is a complete sentence.

Ms. Tucker: Yup, that's probably what they would write.

Ms. Tucker writes the task on the board, making sure to not capitalize the first letter so as not to give the answer away.

the wolf is

Ms. Tucker: At the training, they reminded us to check for the content objective. If we want them to explain the character trait, I'm not sure this quite gets it.

Mr. Chen: Hmm. Yes, that is true. This would just ask the students to describe the wolf, but not explain the character trait. We need to change the fragment.

Ms. Tucker: They should use *because* in the sentence in order to explain.

Mr. Chen: What if we give them this fragment?

Mr. Chen writes on the board "is sneaky."

Ms. Tucker chimes in: Let's try it.

Ms. Tucker writes out the anticipated response. She writes, "The wolf is sneaky because he comes up with a deceitful plan."

Mr. Chen: Hmm. Do you really think the students would say that? Some would, but I think I have others who would just write "The wolf is sneaky." And they wouldn't be wrong; that is true, and it's a complete sentence.

Ms. Tucker: I've got it – let's try this! Let's use the fragment "is sneaky because." Then they have to give us both the wolf and the reason in order to repair the fragment! The students might say, "The wolf is sneaky because he wants to trick the pigs." I think that pulls for more explanation than describing for sure.

Mr. Chen: I love it!

Ms. Tucker erases the board and writes the new task:

is sneaky because

Taking the time to work out the student responses allowed Ms. Tucker and Mr. Chen to reevaluate their assignment and to develop an activity that would best meet their assessment needs.

In Vignette B, we show a teacher implementing Combinations in ways that address aspects of quality teaching for multilingual learners. This vignette emphasizes using student discussion and writing as opportunities for formative assessment; it also provides opportunities for students to discuss with peers and verbalize their thinking as they make sense of the language structures they are using in the tasks. It shows how a teacher can use explicit teaching to help students notice the moves and decisions they make when doing Combinations, especially when that leads to deeper sense-making with the content. It also clarifies how a teacher can model the thinking students need to do as they make those decisions.

VIGNETTE B Teaching sentence boundaries to multilingual learners

Ms. Lisa Hernandez's seventh-grade ELA Classroom is reading the text of a 1984 speech made by Cesar Chavez. For the lesson, she wants her students to think about the idea of idealism presented in the speech. After reading and discussing the text in small groups, the students are assigned a task to identify and repair fragments. The task asks students to use the information they learned from the text about Cesar Chavez and his message to his audience.

Ms. Hernandez wants to see if the students can do the task on their own first. A few of her multilingual learners read the items aloud to themselves and then mark which sentence is incomplete. She notices which students are able to complete the task quickly and which students need extra think time.

Then, Ms. Hernandez puts students into assigned pairs to discuss whether they had the same answers in common. Her students collaborate in pairs to discuss their answers and explain why they selected them. She hears a student named Jorge say to his partner, "I think the second one is not a real sentence. It's about the United Farm Workers. But what else?" Ms. Hernandez hears another student, Angelica, explain to her partner, "Unrealistic means… I think it means it's not real. Like in the speech, Cesar Chavez said some people didn't agree with the labor union."

After a few minutes, Ms. Hernandez shows the correct answer on the board to the students. She explains, "The first one has a *who* (the farm workers) and a *what* (be protected). Be protected is a verb, an action. This is a sentence and it tells us what should happen to farm workers. It's a sentence!"

"The second one is not a sentence, it's a fragment. Roberto and Georgie, can you tell us how you fixed the fragment? I want you to show the class how you made it better!" Ms. Hernandez calls on the two students to come up to the board. She presents their papers on the board with a document camera. She asks them questions that require them to explain their thinking to the class.

"How do you know the item is a fragment? What information is missing?" Ms. Hernandez asks. Roberto explains to the class that the sentence was missing a "what." "To do what? We don't know. So we have to fix it."

Ms. Hernandez presses Roberto to show how he repaired the fragment, not just for sentence structure but for its meaning. "Roberto, please show us how you fixed the fragment and what information you added."

Roberto reads his sentence aloud and explains: "The United Farm Workers hoped to protect the labor rights of workers. In the fragment, it doesn't say what the workers hoped for, so I added that to make a sentence."

Ms. Hernandez revoices Roberto's steps and decisions to the class. "When you read your sentences, you want to think: 'Hmm. Is there information missing? Is there a fragment? Do I have to complete it and fix it?'"

"Georgie, how did you fix the fragment?" Ms. Hernandez asks.

Georgie replies, "The sentence wasn't finished." He points to the end of the fragment. "I added to the sentence. [pointing to the sentence] The United Farm Workers hoped to make people's lives better."

Ms. Hernandez continues, "I see Roberto and Georgie both repaired the fragment by adding information at the end of the sentence. What's cool is that they used very different ideas to build their sentences!"

Jorge chimes in, "I like Roberto's because he talks about the labor rights."

Angelica says, "I think Georgie's is good. It makes me feel proud about what Cesar Chavez did. He was an idealist."

Ms. Hernandez claps her hands. "Bravo, class. This was a simple assignment – to fix one sentence. But you came up with a lot of different ways to think about it and that was not simple!"

This vignette shows how a Combinations task is used to teach a particular skill (repairing fragments) concurrently with the conceptual understandings students are learning about Cesar Chavez. Ms. Hernandez does not just assign the task. She facilitates student-to-student discussion about how language works in the task, she models how to think meta-linguistically using the example of the task and she invites students to problem solve and use reasoning to think about how a sentence can be constructed in the context of the ideas they want to express.

This chapter provides teachers with a suite of strategies for teaching sentence boundaries (and, more broadly, how language works in English) in concert with academic content regardless of a student's grade level or level of English language proficiency. In doing so, we turn on its head an idea we have found to be common in educational circles: that students new to English must spend time learning grammar or English language structures before they are ready to engage deeply with academic content. In fact, the opposite is true: providing a mechanism through Combinations to integrate instruction of language with content amplifies the learning of both.

This chapter also highlights the key considerations for teachers in selecting, designing and implementing these strategies, including that they should target students' level of linguistic knowledge; utilize essential academic vocabulary and content and be carefully designed – ideally in conversation with colleagues – to maximize their power in developing sentence and content knowledge. We hope we have also begun to make clear how these, like all Combinations strategies, can and must be differentiated by embedding needed scaffolds, including multilingual entry points, to provide just-right teaching for both language and content according to specific students' needs. (We touch on multilingual entry points across Chapters 4 through 6 but do a deep dive into this topic in Chapter 7.)

Readers should note that while this and the upcoming chapters provide all the information needed to get started and to make great headway with Combinations, those who wish additional support in task design, differentiation and integration with vocabulary instruction and other elements of quality teaching for multilingual learners can access this information and practice at a Combinations training (see footnote 1 in Chapter 2 for more information).

References

Anderson, R. C., Hiebert, E., Scott, J. A., & Wilkinson, I. A. G. (1985). *Becoming a nation of readers: The report of the commission on reading*. National Academy of Education

Chen, X., Li, H., & Gui, M. (2018). Instructional effects of syntactic parsing on Chinese college students' EFL reading rates. *Journal of Education and Training Studies*, 6(11), 176–185. https://doi.org/10.11114/jets.v6i11.3470

Graham, S., & Perin, D. (2007). Writing next: Effective strategies to improve writing of adolescents in middle and high schools – A report to Carnegie corporation of New York. *Alliance for Excellent Education*. https://media.carnegie.org/filer_public/3c/f5/3cf58727-34f4-4140-a014-723a00ac56f7/ccny_report_2007_writing.pdf

Hennessy, N. (2022). Seriously, syntax matters: Critical connections to comprehension [Webinar]. *Core learning*. https://www.corelearn.com/resource-posts/syntax-webinar/

Hillocks Jr, G., & Smith, M. W. (1991). Grammar and usage. *Handbook of Research on Teaching the English Language Arts*, 591, 603.

Rhinehart, L. V., Bailey, A. L., & Haager, D. (2022). Long-term English learners: Untangling language acquisition and learning disabilities. *Contemporary School Psychology*, 1–13. https://doi.org/10.1007/s40688-022-00420-w

Shanahan, T. (2022, August 13). Trying again – what teachers need to know about sentence comprehension. *Shanahan on Literacy*. https://www.shanahanonliteracy.com/blog/trying-again-what-teachers-need-to-know-about-sentence-comprehension#sthash.jW7aBo8A.zkPsAp4D.dpbs

Snow, C. (2002). Reading for understanding: Toward an r&d program in reading comprehension. *Rand Corporation*. https://www.rand.org/pubs/monograph_reports/MR1465.html

Wexler, N. (2022, September 23). To help students read and write, shower some love on the sentence. *Forbes*. https://www.forbes.com/sites/nataliewexler/2022/09/23/to-help-students-read-and-write-shower-some-love-on-the-sentence

5

Hook It Up, Set It Up

The Power of Conjunctions

To meet the academic demands across subject areas that require students to explain, justify, argue and analyze, all students need to be able to comprehend and express conceptual relationships in the content they are learning. Many students require explicit teaching to learn how to do this, even at the level of the sentence.

In this chapter, we build on the work of researchers who have identified a set of core language skills that are significant predictors of academic literacy (Uccelli, 2019). Among these core skills is the ability to recognize and use "academic discourse markers" to express specific relationships between and among ideas (Uccelli et al., 2012). Academic discourse markers operate as signals within and across sentences to communicate nuance, precision and complexity in meaning. They include linguistic structures that help us understand and produce densely packed information, connect ideas logically and organize arguments (Uccelli, 2019). Some examples can be seen in Table 5.1.

Explicit instruction in discourse markers helps students do more than merely describe or report. Students need to learn to use discourse markers to express complexity in written communication since the writer cannot draw upon many of the tools that help convey meaning orally, such as tone, gesture and facial expression. Academic discourse markers make written text complex

Table 5.1 Examples of Academic Discourse Markers

Conclusion markers	ultimately, finally, overall
Transition words	therefore, as a result, in order to, as opposed to, despite, on the other hand
Sequencing words	first, then, next, prior to, initially, during, before, after, until, as soon as
To introduce evidence	for instance, in fact, according to, based on, for this reason
To express inference	might, could, may, it is possible

and sentence writing in particular an act of critical thinking. For example, where oral conversation might imply a connection between two ideas by speaking them one after another (with the listener making the connection that was implied by the juxtaposition), the discourse markers we explain throughout this chapter explicitly designate particular kinds of relationships between two ideas: cause and effect, result or contradiction. This clarity (making precise relationships clear through the use of discourse markers as opposed to requiring them to be inferred, which is often sufficient and preferred in oral communication) is a feature of strong academic writing.

Explicit attention to discourse markers helps students to track conceptual relationships and extract meaning from texts when they read and to convey similar relationships when they speak and write (Duggleby et al., 2016). Being able to identify that "because" sets up a causal relationship between two components leads the reader to first be able to recognize that kind of thinking when reading and then allows the reader to apply this particular kind of thinking to their own expression both orally and in writing. Attending to discourse markers in sentences, therefore, helps students determine and convey the progression of propositions and shades of meaning in each clause and sentence, ultimately building their analytical and communicative prowess (Fillmore & Fillmore, 2012; Kintsch, 2005).

This chapter presents two heavy-hitting strategies involving a subset of high-utility discourse markers – a specific set of conjunctions – that develop students' analytical thinking and expression of complexity simultaneously with academic content.

The first strategy (because, but & so) teaches varied ways to "hook up" ideas within a sentence to express complex thinking. The second (subordinating conjunctions) teaches students to alter how a sentence starts and "set up" particular types of analytical relationships. These sentence-level strategies teach a small set of discourse markers in English that convey a large range of analytical relationships critical to academic literacy.

We want to emphasize that while the strategies presented in this chapter are taught within and operate at the level of the sentence, our purpose and what we believe is accomplished extend beyond the sentence. Our argument, therefore – in this chapter and for all of Combinations – is that sentence-level strategies provide an accessible mechanism through which we develop the capacity for thinking in more sophisticated ways about and expressing sophisticated thinking about academic content. And because it is nuanced *thinking* that is developed, rather than particular thoughts, the capacity for thinking in this way (through understanding and control of the linguistic structures needed to convey that thinking effectively) becomes internalized and is transferable.

What Are the Gaps in Teaching Sentence Complexity to Multilingual Learners, and How Does Our Approach Address It?

Many students who can write a solid sentence still struggle to write sentences that can convey complex relationships about academic content. This is true not only for students learning English, of course. However, it is a particular characteristic commonly found among students considered to be "long-term English learners", those who have received instruction in US schools for six or more years without yet having achieved a level of proficiency in academic English to be reclassified (Olsen, 2010). Often, social and oral language are strong for students determined to be long-term English learners, yet they require significant support to develop academic vocabulary, and to increase complexity of sentence forms, linguistic range and variety in writing

(Schleppegrell and Christie, 2018). The students' writing may be correct but needs to develop sophistication and variety in linguistic structures and communication of ideas. Teachers are often at a loss for how to effectively develop these students' writing and language skills to meet grade-level standards. In our experience, teachers of multilingual learners have strategies for teaching academic vocabulary and for addressing sentence variety and complexity through grammar instruction, yet they are often disappointed by the results. They know students have big ideas and important things to say, but are frustrated that they are not quipped to help students convey their ideas at the level of complexity in thinking students have and can often communicate in their home language. That is, students' complexity in written expression has not caught up with their verbal expression and thinking because they need supportive language structures in English.

Our approach – direct instruction and progressive mastery through deliberate practice (Panero, 2016) in key academic discourse markers at the level of the sentence – provides a way to scaffold and support the expression of complex thinking in English by teaching the associated forms of language and writing simultaneously.

Through SI, we have surfaced a number of counter-intuitive findings related to students' understanding of sentence complexity and what teachers believe about the impediments to linguistic complexity and how to address it. These findings have implications for our understanding of how to develop academic literacy for multilingual learners and help to explain our confidence in our approach.

The first finding is that many students, including but not exclusive to multilingual learners, use conjunctions incorrectly – or do not use them much at all – and still require instruction to develop a solid understanding of the precise meaning of these linguistic structures in English. This was a particularly surprising and illuminating finding of over 50 inquiry teams exploring where learning was getting stuck with varied student populations in New York City high schools (Panero & Talbert, 2013). Team after team identified a similar problem: when the assessment instruments they created to identify precise language and content challenges were granular enough to pinpoint what students needed, it was a solid understanding of the discourse markers themselves – including the specific function of *because* versus *but* versus *so* – that was getting in students' way. For multilingual learners, what has long been thought of as a list of perfunctory words that students can learn from an anchor chart is in fact something that requires deeper learning and explicit teaching in the context of content-based meaning. This was a profound new insight for the many inquiry teams, who saw through inquiry something that had been invisible to them previously: the need to teach specific discourse markers and students' ability to rapidly express more complexity when they were taught them directly. Teachers came to realize they had been working on analytical thinking in longer forms – asking students to compare multiple texts, for example, and to write argumentative essays – but when it came down to it, many of their students did not understand the discourse markers that would allow expression of these complex relationships in the microcosm of a sentence. They came to see how learning these markers at the sentence level supported the understanding and production of these same analytical relationships first in students' sentences and later (with not much of a lift) in compositions.

Another finding from SI has to do with misconceptions teachers have about *why* students struggle to express relationships within and beyond sentences. When New Dorp High School first began implementing SI, the Science Department Chair and her inquiry teams identified students' difficulty expressing scientific relationships orally and in writing as their area of focus. For two years, they worked on developing academic vocabulary to address this problem (Panero & Talbert, 2013). According to their teacher-generated formative assessments, they made headway in developing this knowledge. Students did indeed learn the vocabulary that teachers taught. Vocabulary is of course critically important for multilingual learners – and all teachers must have an intentional plan and design for selecting words to be taught and ensuring they are learned (Graves et al., 2012). And yet, the team found something through SI that surprised and troubled them: even when the students knew the academic vocabulary (based on assessments that told them this) they still struggled to express *the analytical relationships* that the teachers sought. In the third year of inquiry, however, the school had begun to learn how *hook it up* and other Combinations strategies could meet the needs that surfaced across their inquiry teams schoolwide. When they subsequently implemented the *hook it up* strategies addressed in this chapter, the teams were thrilled to find – suddenly – that their focal students were now able to express the relationships the teachers had most sought. First, they noticed a rapid shift in students' writing; shortly after, they also noticed a change in the quantity and quality of students' oral discussion – something they had been working on by, for example, changing the way teachers asked questions, but – up until now – to no effect. By continuing to adapt to student learning needs and using all available strategies, Combinations allowed the teachers to be able to better assess issues and allow students to grow both their writing and oral communication. We describe the strategies that moved students to meet standards for academic literacy in science at New Dorp later in this chapter.

Hook It Up with Because, But & So

The first strategy utilized by New Dorp's science inquiry teams was *because, but & so* (BBS for short). This is a powerful *hook it up* strategy for advancing student thinking, writing and reading comprehension, particularly in supporting their understanding and expression of the relationships among ideas in academic content. One of the wonderful things about it is that teachers find that it improves student writing very quickly! It takes relatively little instructional time, but it packs a powerful punch.

In using BBS, the teacher provides one sentence stem (the start of a sentence) related to content objectives that are critical to what students are learning. The students complete the sentence stem in three different ways, using *because, but & so*, as in the example in Table 5.2.

Note that, like all Combinations strategies, a core challenge is designing a task that tightly aligns with the specific content objective for a particular lesson or unit. And, like with other

Table 5.2 BBS example 1

> **Directions**: Complete the sentences below using because, but & so.
> Billie Holiday was a jazz and blues legend because …
> Billie Holiday was a jazz and blues legend, but …
> Billie Holiday was a jazz and blues legend, so…

strategies, the teacher should be sure the information the student must supply is that which the teacher *most* wishes to assess and to reinforce. In order to gain the maximum benefit from this Combinations strategy (development of language, content and thinking), this must be accomplished *while* pulling for the type of clean sentence we hope most students will ultimately be able to produce independently.

Note in BBS example 2 (Table 5.3) how the anticipated student responses display (a) tight alignment between task and objective – in other words, the completed task provides the teacher with good information from which they can determine whether or not the student has met the specific content objective and (b) that the stems (first portions of sentences) are designed to pull for clean, strong and complex sentences.

To complete these BBS tasks, students must consider different analytical relationships related to the same concept. This stretches their conceptual understanding and generates more variety and specificity in relationships and associations between concepts than an open-ended question about the same topic.

Table 5.3 BBS example 2

> **Content Objective: Students will be able to differentiate between a compound and a mixture.**
> **Directions: Complete the sentence stems below using because, but & so.**
> Compounds and mixtures are similar because…
> Compounds and mixtures are similar, but…
> Compounds and mixtures are similar, so…
> **Anticipated response**:
> *Compounds and mixtures are similar because they both contain two or more elements.*
> *Compounds and mixtures are similar, but the elements in compounds are chemically bonded.*
> *Compounds and mixtures are similar, so chemists need to be careful which they are using.*

This task requires students to consider and to understand the function of each discrete discourse marker in order to produce three different sentences, each with an accurate meaning and relationship.

The fact that students must apply knowledge of three different markers to write about the same content (one stem) is critical in terms of the strategy's ability to develop analytical thinking, rather than just specific thoughts in one instance. Holding the stem constant allows the distinct function of each discourse marker to become visible to students. In this way, it develops their metacognition about language. With sufficient practice, a student internalizes the function of each marker, and thus the capacity for the expression of precise and varied relationships in ways that transfer to new content, situations and modes (reading, writing, speaking and listening).

Once students have mastered BBS, teachers can introduce additional conjunctions that serve similar functions (since, however and therefore), as in Table 5.4. By teaching other discourse markers in a similar fashion, teachers can progressively raise the level of academic discourse. For example, a teacher might advance students' use of discourse markers by asking them to utilize additional markers, as in the example in Table 5.5. Over time, with repeated practice, students increase their linguistic sophistication and fluency in using discourse markers to express analytical thinking and precise relationships. They can use these markers during the revision process to improve their analysis and communication. With a variety of strategies to draw upon,

Table 5.4 Example without sentence stems

Directions: Create three sentences about parasites below. Each sentence should use one of the conjunctions (since, however and therefore) and show what you've learned about parasites.
Parasites / since
Parasites / however
Parasites / therefore

Table 5.5 Example of stems using additional markers for students to complete

- Compounds and mixtures are similar. For this reason, …
- Compounds and mixtures are similar. In fact, …

students can alter their register according to audience and purpose. In these examples (Tables 5.4 and 5.5), students begin to learn that discourse markers express relationships and that they can appear at the beginning or middle of a sentence or as a bridge between sentences. The teacher can also gradually release scaffolds so that more of the sentence is provided independently by the student. As shown in Table 5.4, the teacher provides only a word or phrase and the conjunctions.

Set It Up with Subordinating Conjunctions

When used at the start of a sentence, a subordinating conjunction introduces a clause that, by definition, cannot stand alone because it is *subordinate*, requiring another clause or part of a sentence to complete it. Some of the most common subordinating conjunctions that appear in written academic text (and thus are worthwhile to teach because they will simultaneously support reading comprehension) are shown in Table 5.6.

In this *set it up* strategy, the teacher provides a sentence stem starting with a subordinating conjunction and asks students to supply the rest. By requiring students to complete a sentence that *begins* in this way, the task itself moves students beyond the

Table 5.6 Common subordinating conjunctions

after	before	in order to	unless	as long as	not only… but also	unlike
although	for	once	until	during	either… or…	through
as	even though/ even if	rather than	when	at	neither… nor…	over/under/ underneath
while	if	since	whenever/ wherever	whether	without/ within	despite

production of a simple sentence to one that expresses a relationship. By designing the stem to start with a subordinating conjunction, the strategy directly teaches one way to produce complexity because the linguistic structure of the task calls for it. This is what sets apart this strategy from just any sentence stem provided by a teacher for students to complete. When designed to reinforce key academic content, students learn to use various linguistic structures to express their conceptual understandings as in the example in Table 5.7. After students demonstrate evidence that they are able to consistently and accurately complete sentences starting with subordinating conjunctions, teachers can increase student independence by providing just a concept (word or phrase) and a subordinating conjunction and ask students to supply a full sentence. Then, teachers may ask students to improve their own written work by revising (improving) their sentences by incorporating subordinating conjunctions.

The *set it up* subordinating conjunction tasks build disciplinary literacy, by which we mean knowledge of how language forms work to communicate precise relationships about academic and discipline-specific content. While the expression of relationships at the level of the sentence may seem to some

Table 5.7 Example of providing students with a concept and subordinating conjunction

Directions: Complete the sentences below based on pg 114–117 of *The Autobiography of Malcolm X*. **Be sure to punctuate where necessary**.
Whenever there is segregation
Before the 1935 Harlem Riot
After the 1935 Harlem Riot

readers to be a low bar in terms of our expectations for students' expression of complexity, through SI we have found that many students do not know how these discourse markers function and that teaching them within the microcosm of the sentence is an effective and efficient way to develop this knowledge. In doing so, teachers develop for students the underpinnings needed to read and express complexity in longer forms.

What *Hook It Up* and *Set It Up* Strategies Do for Students and Teachers

Academic literacy – as distinct from other forms of literacy – is something that must be taught. All writers, in particular, need to learn the structures and forms that support the expression of academic thinking in writing, so as to move from simple reporting to analysis. The *hook it up* and *set it up* strategies that we present in this chapter allow students to be taught the linguistic moves underlying the expression of academic thinking directly and explicitly in connection with – and in ways that accelerate and amplify – the learning of academic content. The strategies we describe support the development of content knowledge, vocabulary acquisition, written and oral expression and reading comprehension simultaneously. Together, the strategies presented in this chapter create a foundation on which other complex academic discourse markers and linguistic practices in written expression of disciplinary content can be learned. Students gain a deep and internalized understanding of how complex sentences are built at a micro level that can then inform their understanding of how language is used in complex texts at the macro level. For students, the *hook it up* and *set it up* strategies are a gateway to a vast range of rhetorical expressions and ways of analytical thinking that provide the foundation multilingual learners need for academic success.

For content teachers, the *hook it up* and *set it up* strategies provide a way to teach content simultaneously and to also support multilingual learners to build the linguistic practices needed for high levels of content learning and disciplinary thinking.

For language development specialists, these strategies provide a way to explicitly and efficiently teach how language works without having to do so in ways that feel divorced from meaningful content learning. These strategies allow all teachers to learn a lot about what their students understand and how they think about the content they are teaching. They illuminate gaps in content knowledge and skill that were often masked by tasks that did not assess content and language learning together, or by assessments that never got small (specific) enough to pay such close attention to language. Teachers are able to more clearly see what multilingual learners are able to do and how they engage in disciplinary thinking because the tasks are granular. Teachers are also able to see very specifically what specific conjunction, vocabulary or mechanics students need to learn next based on how they respond to the tasks. The tasks function like a microscope – illuminating and making visible problem areas that could not be seen with a more removed, distant assessment.

In summary, the strategies provide a way for teachers to integrate all that is being asked of them; to do so in a way that is highly impactful (that accelerates student learning) within a relatively short instructional time and in ways that pinpoint needed teaching points.

Design and Teaching Tips

Like all Combinations strategies, these are harder to design than they look. What's difficult is becoming extremely precise about the most pressing objectives for language and content, and designing the task (a) to pull for the content and thinking from the student that is related to that objective (rather than providing that part of the content in the task itself) and (b) to pull for the kind of clean and complex sentence you hope the students will come to produce independently. The criteria for a solid task, then, is not whether it's possible for a student to complete it correctly but, rather, whether it pulls for a clean and complex sentence about the critical content.

As with all Combinations strategies, teachers should integrate all aspects of quality instruction for multilingual learners, including the critical importance of student collaboration and conversation and valuing and drawing upon varied entry points to make the work accessible and develop both language and content simultaneously. A wonderful thing about Combinations is that the strategies are easily adjusted to include a range of entry points, providing access to the same rigorous content regardless of a student's level of English language proficiency. While we take a deep dive into multilingual entry points with Combinations in Chapter 7, below we illustrate two of the key entry points we have also discussed in earlier chapters: (a) the use of home language as an asset and resource and (b) the use of the needed level of language scaffolding. The following tips apply to both *hook it up* and *set it up* strategies (and to all Combinations). Students may benefit from the entry points listed in Figure 5.1, especially if they are newcomers, have learning differences, experienced interrupted schooling or struggle with attention issues. Therefore, tasks need to be further broken down into component parts in explicit ways to then integrate and build up to composite skills through progressive mastery through the teacher's deliberate practice (Panero, 2016).

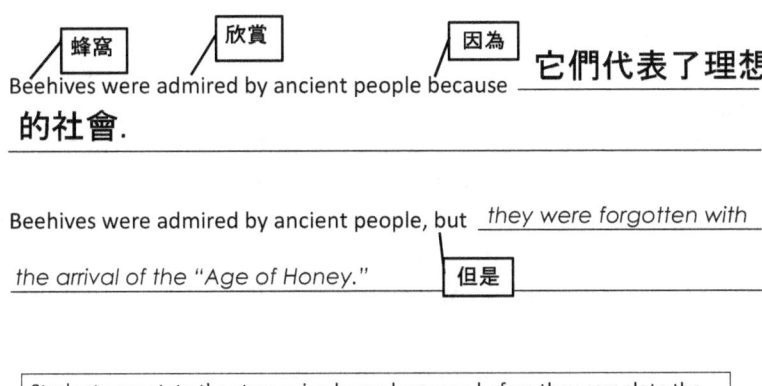

FIGURE 5.1 Example of students responding to sentence stems in their home language before writing a response in English.

Figure 5.1 shows how to build on and use students' home language as a resource with a BBS task. In this case, the teacher did not know the student's home language, but told the student to annotate the stem in English or their home language before completing it. Students may need a direct explanation of the correlating conjunctions with similar meanings or functions that are used in their home language (e.g., *but* in English is *pero* in Spanish and 可是 in Chinese). Multilingual learners will benefit from knowing the equivalent word or phrase used in their language to communicate the same relationship. Teachers should support students to compare the conjunctions used in English and those used in their home language to link ideas and connect relationships in the same way. Teachers should provide students time to annotate the provided sentence stems in their home language and/or in English so that they understand the nature of the relationship they need to articulate (see Figure 5.1). Students can also use their home language to discuss the conceptual relationships in the task.

Some students also need additional access and support. Teachers can consider asking students to complete the sentence with only one of the conjunctions at a time, rather than three or more at a time, as in Figure 5.2. Or this can be a receptive task (see Figure 5.3). Teachers should remember these are temporary scaffolds, as students will further develop an understanding of the English language and specifically an understanding of the conjunctions through the use of all three with the same stem as in Figure 5.3.

Overall, give yourself time and space to develop these tasks. It might take longer than you expect to develop a task that does everything you wish for: that pulls for and reinforces important content *while* teaching students to produce the kind of complex sentence that will yield so many benefits. It's best to create these with one or more colleagues; to write the anticipated student responses (what you expect a student would produce when faced with the task) and to tweak the activity until you get it right, as in the following vignette of a co-teaching pair working together to design a task that truly aligns with their instructional objective (see Vignette A).

>
> **Word Box**
> decomposer   consumer   producer

A snake is a _consumer_ because _it eats rabbits, grasshoppers and mice._

A tree is a _producer_ because _it gets energy from the sun._

A mushroom is a _decomposer_ because _it gets energy from dead grass and seeds._

FIGURE 5.2 Example of student response when provided with only one conjunction at a time.

>
> 1. **Read** the sentences below.
> 2. **Circle** the connecting word (because, but or so).
> 3. **Underline** the key ideas in each sentence.
> 4. **Talk** with a partner. What do the sentences tell us about Billie Holiday?

Billie Holiday is a jazz and blues legend because her phrasing and vocal stylings were unique.

Billie Holiday is a jazz and blues legend, but many young people today do not know her music.

Billie Holiday is a jazz and blues legend, so everyone should listen to her music.

Task is *receptive*.

FIGURE 5.3 Example of a receptive task for students to review conjunctions and analyze the text.

VIGNETTE A

Ms. de Leon and Mr. Andrews co-teach a ninth-grade global history class together. They just finished planning their week of lessons on the Haitian Revolution and are sitting down to create the Combinations tasks that students will do aligned to the lessons' content objectives. Students have already been introduced to both the *hook it up* and *set it up* strategies. Ms. de Leon and Mr. Andrews want students to know how to use the conjunctions well so they can use them in the upcoming essay about the factors that led to the success of the Haitian Revolution. They plan to provide frequent practice using the content from the unit in the lessons leading up to the essay.

Ms. de Leon: Based on this week's lessons, we really want students to explain the cause and effect relationships in the Haitian Revolution. We don't want them to just recount what happened but to explain what factors led to the success of the revolution.

Mr. Andrews: I took a stab at a few sentence stems last night actually. Let's see if these work for our lessons.

Directions: Complete the following sentence stems using information you have learned about the Haitian Revolution.
Before the Haitian Revolution, ...
After the insurgents led the assault at Saint Domingue,
   ...
Even though Napoleon tried to re-establish slavery in Haiti, ...

Ms. de Leon: I think these stems definitely get the students to think about the content. Let's try writing the anticipated responses.

Ms. de Leon and Mr. Andrew imagine what they expect their students would write together. They think aloud and then write what they think students would answer:

Before the Haitian Revolution, *enslaved people planted sugar and coffee.*

After the insurgents led the assault at Saint Domingue, *many plantations were burned.*

Even though Napoleon tried to re-establish slavery in Haiti, *he was not successful.*

Mr. Andrew:	I'm glad we tried that out. Now, I am not so sure.
Ms. de Leon:	Not sure about what? What are you thinking?
Mr. Andrew:	I feel like these three sentences kind of just require students to describe what happened.
Ms. de Leon:	I see what you're saying. I think it's because we are using the conjunctions "before" and "after" so it makes sense that the sentences are describing the sequence of events, but not necessarily showing the cause and effect.
Mr. Andrew:	I am hoping for a task that gets students to think more about what contributed to the success of the revolution.
Ms. de Leon:	Okay let's try working backwards from what you want. Can you give me an example? What would you want the students to write? What's an example of an answer that looks like what you have in mind?
Mr. Andrew:	I want them to explain the things that contributed to the success of the revolution.
Ms. de Leon:	Okay great, like what exactly?
Mr. Andrew:	Well, for example, something like... [Mr. Andrew writes down]

The revolutionaries gathered to strategize in order to plan the rebellion.

The insurgents became very powerful since they collected weapons.

They made sure they could maintain their freedom.

They faced a lot of challenges, but they persevered.

Ms. de Leon: Oh look, when you said that, you used "in order to" and "since". Let's use that. And let's come up with some other examples, based on what you wrote down.

After discussing and trying out a few different stems, the two teachers drafted the following task:

> **Directions: Complete the following sentence stems using information you have learned about the Haitian Revolution.**
>
> In order to rebel against enslavement, …
>
> Since the insurgents gathered an army and weapons, …
>
> In order to maintain their freedom, …
>
> Although it was not easy to get emancipation, …
>
> Despite resistance from white planters and merchants, …

They wrote out the following anticipated responses for each stem and saw that the resulting sentences would indeed get students to think about cause and effect and not just describe a sequence of events.

Anticipated responses:

> *In order to rebel against enslavement, the enslaved people planned and strategized together.*
>
> *Since the insurgents gathered an army and weapons, Napoleon could not defeat them.*
>
> *In order to maintain their freedom, the revolutionaries continued to plant sugar and coffee.*
>
> *Although it was not easy to get emancipation, the Haitian revolution was a success.*
>
> *Despite resistance from white planters and merchants, the revolutionaries fought for liberty.*

Vignette B illustrates a teacher integrating varied aspects of quality instruction to maximize the power of Combinations in their instruction. Specifically, notice how this teacher, Mr. Hernandez, uses formative assessment in an ongoing way throughout the lesson – both for oral conversation and student writing – to identify and nail down needed teaching points.

VIGNETTE B

Mr. Jaime Hernandez is a fifth-grade teacher in Queens, NY. Students in his classroom represent speakers of over a dozen languages. They are all orally fluent in English but have not been reclassified as English learners. Mr. Hernandez is hoping to improve the students' writing about academic topics they are learning in social studies. After learning about diseases that were introduced to the Western Hemisphere, Mr. Hernandez asked his students to complete a BBS task.

> Diseases were introduced to the Western Hemisphere because …
>
> Diseases were introduced to the Western Hemisphere, but …
>
> Diseases were introduced to the Western Hemisphere, so …

Students discussed the stems together before committing their ideas to paper. Mr. Hernandez heard a lot of students chiming in with ideas and felt proud that the students got the content right. He collected the student papers and reviewed each student's sentences, checking to see if their sentences worked with each conjunction. He found that 60% of his class wrote sentences that did not quite fit when using the conjunction *so*.

One student wrote: "Diseases were introduced to the Western Hemisphere so the colonizers brought the germs". Another student wrote: "Diseases were introduced to the

Western Hemisphere so the diseases were bad". Mr. Hernandez couldn't quite tell if those two students could name the negative consequences resulting from the diseases. Mr. Hernandez wondered if the students really knew how to explain the cause and effect relationship using *so*.

He remembered hearing at a Combinations training that students often struggle with "so" tasks. Since it indicates the relationship of cause and effect, a more complex relationship is signaled compared to *because* or *but*. He knew it would take some more direct instruction with his students.

The next day, he led a conversation with students about it. He showed them a clear example of how to use *so* using everyday content that students would understand to ensure they got the function of the conjunction: It is raining, *so* I will bring an umbrella. Then, he told the students to use the same way of thinking to think about what happened as a result of the diseases being brought to the West. He provided three ways to complete the stem, only one of which was a clean sentence using *so* as intended (sentence A).

A) Diseases were introduced to the Western Hemisphere, so many indigenous people died from illness.
B) Diseases were introduced to the Western Hemisphere, so the diseases were brought from Europe.
C) Diseases were introduced to the Western Hemisphere, so they brought a new culture also.

"Students, all three sentences use *so* but only one of them shows cause and effect. Can you talk to your partner and discuss which sentence uses *so* to show a result? That shows cause and effect using *so*?" Mr. Hernandez asked his students to discuss for two minutes in pairs as he listened in.

"I heard a lot of you paying really close attention to the sentence and how to use the word *so*. The best sentence using *so* is sentence A. Ana, tell me why it's not sentence B".

Ana repeated what she told her partner. "Sentence B doesn't tell what happened after the diseases came to the west. The right way is to say what happened after and to use the *so*".

Jorge chimed in, "It's wrong because the second part of the sentence is just repeating the same thing!"

Mr. Hernandez extended the conversation. "That's right. We want to use *so* when we want to show a result – like a before and after effect. Who can tell me what might be wrong with sentence C?"

Jimmy read the whole sentence aloud for the class. Then, he said, "I think the new culture came with the disease but that doesn't show a result from what happened with the disease".

Mr. Hernandez said, "Thank you Ana, Jorge, and Jimmy for your insights. Sentence A is the only one that uses *so* to show a result or a cause and effect relationship. I want you to think about this the next time I ask you to write a sentence using *so*. I am going to keep these examples on the wall for you to see and collect more examples from you in the future until we get this right!"

Closing

BBS and subordinating conjunctions are among the most popular strategies we have seen during the course of our work with teachers using Combinations. Content teachers often first pick up these strategies not because they want to teach language but because they want to assess content understanding. Then they find they have been inadvertently teaching language without an explicit intention to do so and are now providing students with an accessible and routine way to think about how language is used in their expression of disciplinary thinking. This is a testament to the potential of Combinations to shift teachers' understanding of what it means to teach language and content simultaneously. Through the *hook it up* and *set it up* strategies, teachers can experience how exactly teaching language is critical to teaching content. Even more important, perhaps, is the power of these strategies in developing the linguistic underpinnings that allow for and support analytical thinking.

References

Duggleby, S. J., Tang, W., & Kuo-Newhouse, A. (2016). Does the use of connective words in written assessments predict high school students' reading and writing achievement? *Reading Psychology, 37*(4), 511–532. http://dx.doi.org/10.1080/02702711.2015.1066910

Fillmore, L. W., & Fillmore, C. J. (2012). What does text complexity mean for English learners and language minority students. *Understanding language: Language, literacy, and learning in the content areas* (pp. 64–74). Stanford University.

Graves, M. F., August, D., & Mancilla-Martinez, J. (2012). *Teaching vocabulary to English language learners*. Teachers College Press.

Kintsch, W. (2005). An overview of top-down and bottom-up effects in comprehension: The ci perspective. *Discourse Processes, 39*(2–3), 125–128.

Olsen, L. (2010). *Reparable harm: Fulfilling the unkept promise of educational opportunity for California's long term English learners*. Californians Together. https://web.stanford.edu/~hakuta/Courses/Ed330X%20Website/Olsen_ReparableHarm2ndedition.pdf

Panero, N. S. (2016). Progressive mastery through deliberate practice: A promising approach for improving writing. *Improving Schools, 19*(3), 229–245.

Panero, N. S., & Talbert, J. E. (2013). *Strategic inquiry: Starting small for big results in education*. Harvard Education Press.

Schleppegrell, M., & Christie, F. (2018). Linguistic features of writing development: A functional perspective. In Bazerman, C., Applebee, A., Berninger V., Brandt, D., Graham, S., Jeffery, J., Matsuda, P. K., Murphy, S., Rowe, D. W., Schleppegrell, M., & Wilcox, K. C., *The lifespan development of writing* (pp. 111–150). NCTE.

Uccelli, P. (2019). Learning the language for school literacy: Research insights and a vision for a crosslinguistic research program. I. V. Grøver, P. Uccelli, ML Rowe, & E. Lieven (Eds.), *Learning through language: Towards an educationally informed theory of language learning* (pp. 95–109). Cambridge University Press. http://dx.doi.org/10.1017/9781316718537.010

Uccelli, P., Dobbs, C. L., & Scott, J. (2012). Mastering academic language: Organization and stance in the persuasive writing of high school students. *Written Communication*, *30*(1), 36–62. http://dx.doi.org/10.1177/0741088312469013

6

Stretch It

Expansion, Appositives, Combining and Parallel Revision

Academic literacy can be defined as the ability to understand and to express complex conceptual and academic relationships through language. Its development, therefore, rests equally upon an understanding of the linguistic elements used to express particular relationships *and* on the academic content within which these relationships gain meaning. The linguistic structures and academic content need each other to make sense; they are intertwined. Thus, the teaching of both must be intertwined as well.

In Chapter 5, we presented strategies for understanding and expressing varied relationships between two ideas within a sentence (cause and effect, result, contradiction and subordination). In this chapter, we raise the level of complexity, introducing a second set of strategies for developing students' ability to understand and express relationships between and among multiple ideas, all in relation to a single sentence kernel. We call the strategies we present in this chapter – expansion, appositives, combining and parallel revision – *stretch* strategies because they teach students directly and explicitly what types of additional information to include and how to include it to produce more information-rich sentences. In doing so, stretch strategies also teach how densely packed information can be understood when reading. In various ways, these strategies provide practice in identifying a sentence kernel (its skeleton) versus information that has been layered on top of the kernel to adjust its meaning. In solidifying students' understanding of what constitutes the kernel, what constitutes the additional information and how the syntactical arrangement of all elements affects meaning, these strategies support high-level comprehension and communication.

What Challenges in Sentence Complexity Do Stretch Strategies Help to Address?

To effectively deduce meaning from and produce meaning with academic language in English, students need a solid understanding of how sentences in English function. They need a solid understanding not only of what is and is not a sentence (see Chapter 4), but also of how to determine what the sentence is primarily about. In other words, they must be able to identify, without necessarily knowing these terms, the subject and predicate (the unelaborated skeleton that forms the sentence kernel), or else they may become lost in description and confused about meaning.

In "A Case for the Sentence in Reading Comprehension", Cheryl Scott (2009) identifies this problem, including the challenge in correctly identifying the subject and predicate (and thus the meaning) when a sentence is long, densely packed or when the subject and predicate are distant from one another. Consider the confusion that could occur, for example, in the following sentence from *The Washington Post*:

> Anthony S. Fauci, the nation's preeminent infectious-disease expert who achieved unprecedented fame while enduring withering political attacks as the face of the coronavirus pandemic response under two presidents, plans to step down in December after more than a half-century of public service, he announced Monday.
>
> (Abutaleb, 2022)

Indeed, we found this to be the case through our Strategic Inquiry work. After drilling down to identify challenges in reading comprehension, then more narrowly in context clues and comma use, many teams discovered a misconception that interfered with reading comprehension. Many of the studied students knew commas separate items in a list, but did not know that commas are also used to set off noun clauses, as in the appositive structure, where a noun phrase restates a prior noun. (The sentence from *The Washington Post* includes one very long appositive.) This was a surprising and exciting discovery, since the teachers had no idea their students held this misconception, much less that it was a pattern. Once they became aware of this pattern, they could directly teach to it; the teachers quickly found that when students learned to produce sentences with appositives, they were better able to understand sentences that included them when they read.

Many students, including those learning English, struggle both to produce sentences with densely packed information and to make sense of them in academic texts when they read. The strategies in this chapter provide direct instruction in the linguistic moves used to create dense sentences in English, thus lifting the veil about how precisely to exhibit and to develop academic literacy. Like all of Combinations, stretch strategies combine the teaching of language with content to accelerate the learning of both while developing metacognition, the ability to think about thinking. Through practice, students learn the function of the linguistic moves they are learning and thus become able to apply them independently in new situations.

Expansion: The Ultimate Stretch Strategy

In this strategy, the most direct for teaching students to distinguish the skeleton of a sentence from its other elements, a student is provided with a kernel (a simple unelaborated sentence) and questions to answer in relation to the kernel drawn from *who, what, when, where, why* and *how*. First, students provide answers to the questions posed. Then, they use all the information from the kernel and their answers to write an expanded sentence, as

> **Simple sentence: They conduct electricity.**
>
> **What?** _metallic solids_
>
> **When?** _in the solid or liquid phases_
>
> **Why?** _because they contain mobile electrons_
>
> **Expanded sentence:**
>
> _Metallic solids conduct electricity in the solid or liquid phases because they contain mobile electrons._

FIGURE 6.1 Example of student work where the student uses information from the kernel and their answers to write an expanded sentence.

in the example in Figure 6.1. The teacher's task is in bold and student responses are in italics.

Note that expansion tasks are highly controlled by the teacher. Each task is carefully designed to pull for specific content and to teach, through the task's carefully controlled design, how the pieces of additional information can be put together properly, in what order, and efficiently in relation to a kernel of an English sentence. The students should not leave out information or supply additional information.

It is trickier than it looks to create a simple kernel that pulls for (rather than providing within the kernel itself) the most essential content, that which the teacher most wishes the students to supply. The teacher must also consider the level of linguistic complexity she wishes to require. We strongly recommend that a teacher begin with one to two question words only, always sitting in the seat of an imagined student as you design and test your activity (preferably with one or more colleagues) to make sure it pulls both for the content and sentence writing that you want. This usually takes a few revisions. The question you should ask yourself when designing is not whether it's *possible* for students to complete the task, but rather whether the task as designed is likely to pull for the information you want in the way that you want it, with the kind of sentence you hope students will come to produce independently.

One way to generate a kernel is to start with the end in mind, to imagine an expanded sentence you hope students would write and then eliminate information leaving only the kernel. You can then decide which questions to ask (what additional information you would like students to supply). Note that you should not expect students to produce the exact sentence you started with. You wrote that sentence just to get to your kernel! Ideally, there are multiple ways to expand the kernel correctly (students should not have to read the teacher's mind). The following initially-expanded sentence provides an example of getting to the kernel by crossing out detail:

> Anthony S. Fauci, ~~the nation's preeminent infectious-disease expert who achieved unprecedented fame while enduring withering political attacks as the face of the coronavirus pandemic response under two president,~~ plans to step down ~~in December after more than a half-century of public service, he announced Monday.~~

Once the kernel is deduced (Anthony S. Fauci plans to step down), you can consider tweaking it. Notice in the example (Figure 6.2) how one small change in the kernel (replacing "He" with "Anthony Fauci") makes a big difference in the level of complexity required for both content and skill, even when the question words remain the same.

To select question words, the teacher moves from left to right in the sentence kernel, interrogating the kernel as she goes. Given the kernel "They conduct electricity", for example (See Figure 6.1),

Kernel Option 1 (Pulls for less information and a less complex sentence structure than Option 2.)	Kernel Option 2 (Pulls for more information and a more complex sentence structure than Option 1.)
Kernel: He plans to step down. Who? . . . . When? . . . . Anticipated student response: *Anthony Fauci plans to step down in December.*	Anthony Fauci plans to step down. Who? . . . . When? . . . . Anticipated student response: *Anthony Fauci, the nation's preeminent infection disease expert, plans to step down in December.* *Note that the design of this Option Two task pulls for an appositive. Therefore, this design is only appropriate after the appositive structure has been taught to students.

FIGURE 6.2 Example of two options for student responses when provided with a kernel sentence.

the teacher might ask herself: *what* conducts electricity? If she wishes this question to be answered, she would put *what* as her first question word. *When*, she might ask next, and so on. The order of the question words provided follows the order in which it is logical to ask particular questions when reading the simple sentence.

In teaching expansion, students can first learn to build their sentences in a similar way by following the order of the questions about the kernel as presented in the task. As students become proficient, they can learn to vary the order in which they present information in their expanded sentences. "Look at this neat trick", a teacher might say. "You can start your expanded sentence with the *when* or the *why*, as in 'In the solid or liquid phases, metallic solids conduct electricity because they contain mobile electrons.' Or 'Because they contain mobile electrons, metallic solids conduct electricity in the solid or liquid phases.'" Students can discuss the distinct emphases of each variation, and the subtle but important impact of their linguistic decisions on meaning. Also, students learn that in starting sentences with *when, why or how* they are producing forms that appear more frequently in written than in oral language. In learning to produce such structures they are better able to understand them, and the shades of meaning they convey, when they read.

For multilingual learners, expansion provides students with many opportunities to think about linguistic form and function in the context of complex ideas and relationships. Multilingual learners learn how to build information-dense sentences when they come to understand the functions of words and phrases within a sentence and how they can be arranged to express ideas in increasingly complex ways. Expansion is the most direct strategy we have come across that does so, with a focus on language at the sentence level, without having to sacrifice the students' attention to content and thinking.

Appositives

Our second stretch strategy is to teach students to write sentences using appositives. An appositive is a noun or noun phrase that follows another noun or noun phrase to provide additional information, explanation or a definition. Appositives are set off by commas – or sometimes dashes or parentheses – within a sentence. The appositive is an especially useful grammatical term and concept to teach in terms of its function because it allows students to pack additional information in their own writing and to understand this form when they read, directly addressing the misconception that commas only separate items in a list, as described earlier. In addition, it is a wonderful strategy for reinforcing and assessing content.

The appositive strategy can teach multilingual learners directly that syntactic complexity can have a significant impact on meaning. The arrangement and order of words and punctuation in the sentence are linked to its meaning and function. The appositive strategy teaches this fundamental aspect of language not through abstract rules or grammatical concepts but in ways that are intertwined with meaning – so that the linguistic structures support thinking and understanding especially for students who are learning English as a new language.

Like all of Combinations, the appositive strategy can be more or less scaffolded, as the examples in Figure 6.3 indicate. The first row provides examples of more and less scaffolded appositives activities in social studies; the second row in mathematics.

Combining

Our third stretch strategy, combining, is one of the most researched strategies found to improve both grammar and sentence writing (Graham & Perin, 2007; Saddler, 2012). In a nutshell, this strategy involves presenting two or more sentences to students and asking them to combine them into one. This is a particularly powerful strategy for students learning English, because, when carefully designed, combining activities can target specific English language features that teachers wish to teach and reinforce (such as pronouns) as well as pulling for application of language forms learned earlier. For example, if students have learned *because, but & so* through Combinations scaffolds, they can now be asked to

Stretch It ◆ 99

◀──────── More Scaffolded   Less Scaffolded ────────▶

Directions: Based on your knowledge of Harriet Tubman, match each appositive to its subject.

1. Harriet Tubman	___ a network of secret routes and safe houses,
2. The Underground Railroad	___ the conflict fought between the southern and northern U.S. states,
3. the Civil War	___ a formerly enslaved person and conductor for the Underground Railroad,
4. Araminta "Minty" Ross	___ the people who Tubman led to the north,
5. escapees	___ the name given to Tubman at birth,

Directions: Based on your knowledge of Harriet Tubman, fill in the blank using an appositive.

Harriet Tubman, _____, escaped from slavery in 1849 and led other slaves to freedom before the Civil War.

Harriet Tubman, _____, led other slaves to freedom before the Civil War.

Directions: Based on your knowledge of Harriet Tubman, write a sentence with the given appositive.

Appositive: a network of secret routes and safe houses

_____

Appositive: the people who led Harriet Tubman to the North

_____

Appositives (matching)

1. chord	___ a line segment that passes through the center of a circle,
2. tangent	___ a set of points equidistant from a given point,
3. secant	___ a line segment inside a circle with endpoints on the circle,
4. diameter	___ a segment or line that touches a circle at one point only,
5. circle	___ an angle whose vertex is at the center of a circle,
6. central angle	___ a line segment that touches a circle at two points,

Angle A, <u>an acute angle</u>, measures less than 90 degrees.
Angle B, <u>a right angle</u>, measures exactly 90 degrees.
Angle C, <u>an obtuse angle</u>, measures greater than 90 degrees.
Angle D, <u>a straight angle</u>, measures exactly 180 degrees.
Angle E, <u>a reflex angle</u>, measures greater than 180 degrees.

Given a topic

Topic: acute angle

Figure A, <u>an acute angle</u>, is less than ninety degrees.

Topic: obtuse angle

Figure C, <u>an obtuse angle</u>, is more than ninety degrees.

FIGURE 6.3 Examples of a continuum of scaffolding – Appositives.
Social studies examples courtesy of Laura Rivera.

recognize the need for these words and to apply this knowledge in combining provided sentences (Hebert et al., 2018). In requiring students to pay very close attention to language and word sequence in sentences – and specifically how to use language concisely and efficiently to best convey the needed information in a combined sentence – combining teaches the skills and habits of mind underlying the revision process in writing within an accessible (small) format.

We considered calling combining a *shrink* rather than a *stretch* strategy, because students begin with multiple sentences that they must combine into one. What combining actually requires, however, is for students to identify the common kernel that can be created across sentences and to expand it on their own by pulling from both. Students should be expected to draw upon strategies they have learned previously when they combine. Therefore, combining represents a move forward in the gradual release of scaffolds toward student independence. If they have learned to use the word *so* in the more scaffolded BBS strategy, for example, they can then be asked to apply it in a Combinations task, as in the example in Figure 6.4. To combine the two sentences in this example correctly, students must recognize the relationship implied across sentences and apply their knowledge of the function of the conjunction *so* to make this relationship explicit in their own new (combined) sentence.

When the student is able to make such complex sentences, they are able to put more information into a smaller package, a smaller delivery space, creating a more complex idea. For example, in the

Directions: Combine the sentences below.

- Frederick Douglass knew he wouldn't convince a Southern audience.
- Frederick Douglass wrote his autobiography to target a Northern audience.

Frederick Douglass knew he wouldn't convince a Southern audience, so he wrote his autobiography to target a Northern one.

FIGURE 6.4 Example of a student taking two sentences and combining them into one.

expanded sentence in Figure 6.4, we now have more than the facts that Douglass knew he wouldn't convince a Southern audience, and, separately, that Douglass wrote an autobiography to target a Northern audience; we now have the *reason* he did so made clear. Making this relationship explicit (rather than implied, as is often sufficient in oral language) is a feature of academic writing. Learning how to produce such sentences will also help students make meaning of them when they read.

The transfer of oral language to written expression is a process that all students need, facilitated through direct and explicit instruction of how to construct sentences, even more so for students who are learning to do so in a new language. Such syntactic moves are automatic for skilled writers, sometimes executed without a lot of direct attention. Yet these critical moves used to reformulate, manipulate and improve sentences are not transparent to students who are still learning the structures that govern the use of the new language. Sentence combining helps break down each of the moves into micro steps, pulling the curtain back to reveal how sentences are constructed in order to improve communicative efficacy and complexity.

The challenge (again) is in creating a task that pulls for essential content knowledge *while* providing application and practice of just-right, sentence-level skills. Combining activities can range from the very simple to the extremely complex. We recommend starting with two sentences, and bringing additional sentences into the activities gradually. As always, be sure to sit in the seat of your imagined students and try the activities before you finalize them.

A note on the use of home language with the combining strategy in particular. Since this activity specifically targets and develops the use of English syntax, it is not necessary to ask students to complete combining tasks in their home language. That is, combining sentences in the home language will help students express the ideas in a combined sentence but will not give students the opportunity to practice manipulating words and phrases to precisely communicate those ideas *in English* (the whole point of the strategy). The point is to give students opportunities to work with the given sentences in English and figure out the syntactic choices they can make to complete the task. However, it may be beneficial for multilingual learners to talk in their home language as they process their thinking and approach the problem of how best to combine.

For those interested in a deeper dive into the topic, we recommend Bruce Saddler's 2012 book *A Teacher's Guide to Improving Sentence Writing*, which focuses entirely on varied uses and impacts of sentence combining.

Parallel Revision

Parallel revision is a critical stretch strategy for ensuring that skills learned in tightly controlled Combinations activities transfer to students' independent writing. Note that while parallel revision may look like a paragraph-level strategy since students are working to improve a simple, correct but boring paragraph, it is in fact a sentence-level one; its purpose is to solidify students' understanding of the linguistic moves that writers use in crafting complex sentences. Its core purpose, in other words, is to develop metacognition and metalinguistic awareness.

In parallel revision, the teacher crafts a simple correct but boring paragraph (one with many sentence kernels) and provides specific directions for improving it, drawing upon the sentence strategies that have been taught. This provides an opportunity for students to apply knowledge learned in discrete and more highly controlled Combinations tasks to improving (not correcting) a given paragraph. After students learn to improve a given paragraph in this way, teachers can ask students to apply these same skills to improving their own and/or their classmates' writing.

The key in teaching parallel revision is that the teacher models how to annotate the paragraph to illuminate their thinking about how to improve it. The teacher thinks out loud, sharing with students how they might interrogate (ask questions about) the kernels, making her metalinguistic thinking visible to students. The teacher emphasizes different questions that could be asked, showing that there is no one right way to improve each sentence and the paragraph overall, but rather demonstrating to students how to draw upon varied options based on previously learned skills and the content or information that needs to be added. As the teacher shares her thinking aloud, she inserts her selected questions as annotations in a format that all students can see. These annotations become directions to follow to improve the simple paragraph, as shown in Figure 6.5. In this example, second-grade students have been studying the ocean.

As shown in Figure 6.6, the teacher led the entire class to follow the directions provided by the annotations. Together, they co-constructed the improved paragraph.

The power of parallel revision for students who are learning English is that it teaches them the function of linguistic structures within the context of a short text using the content they are learning. Like all Combinations strategies, students learn linguistic form and function simultaneously with meaningful content and ideas. Parallel revision requires students to do this in the context of a coherent paragraph, a set of ideas that are connected and explanatory. Rather than haphazardly adding words and phrases to expand a composition, students use parallel revision to consider linguistic form and function intertwined

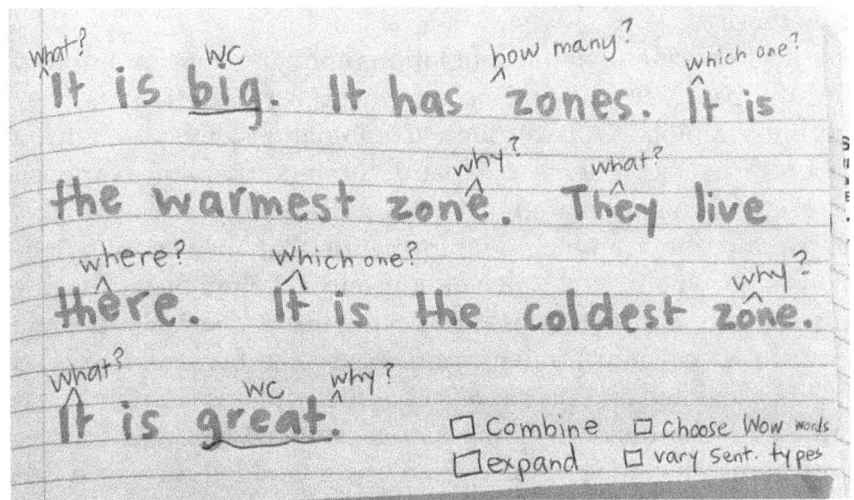

FIGURE 6.5 Example of a teacher thinking aloud and adding her questions as annotations for students to then improve a simple paragraph.

104 ◆ Getting into the Work

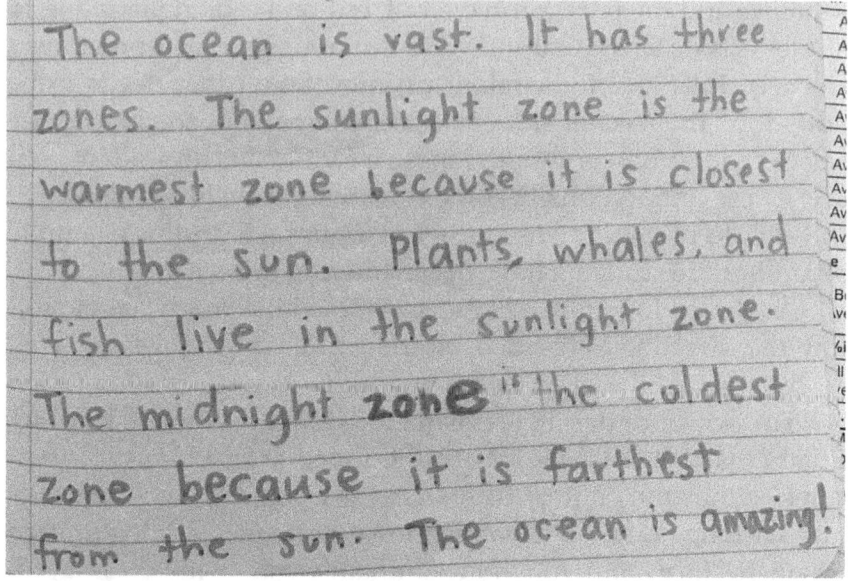

FIGURE 6.6 Example of student work where the teacher led the entire class in following the directions provided by the annotations. Together, they developed the improved paragraph.

with the critical ideas they want to communicate about content and they also learn to manipulate language and word order in order to improve their written communication with clarity and coherence.

It's important that the annotations and directions for improving the paragraph should be drawn from what students have become familiar with through Combinations. Once taught, a teacher can ask students to expand, combine, include an appositive, vary sentence starters, etc. Students will have learned that to expand, they can include information that answers the questions who, where, why, when or how and therefore that including these words as annotations is following the teacher's direction to *expand*. We call this strategy *parallel* revision because it should be implemented and practiced in parallel with the Combinations strategies. As soon as a Combinations strategy has been learned sufficiently, it can be applied (in a less scaffolded form as a further push toward independent application) through parallel revision. A teacher provides only the directions (annotations) to which students can reply with strategies that they have learned.

First, the teacher models how to annotate and follow the directions to write the improved paragraph. Gradually, the teacher releases responsibility, first providing annotations/directions and writing the improved paragraph together as a class and then with students following the teacher's directions to write the improved paragraph on their own. When they are ready, students will write their own annotations/directions and follow them to write the new paragraph. It is critical that the teacher and then the students annotate the paragraph with the directions (e.g., the actual question word) rather than with the improved language (e.g., the answer to the question asked). For the first annotation in Figure 6.5, for example, it is critical that the teacher write "what" as her first annotation rather than stating aloud that they can improve the sentence by answering the question "what" and then writing the answer (which would be "ocean") as her annotation. Why do we want to write the question word rather than the answer as the annotation? Because what is most important to teach in parallel revision is the transferable skill of recognizing what is missing or could be improved in terms of *function*. It is this metacognitive and metalinguistic habit and skill of seeing the kernel along with what specifically could and should be added to amplify it that we most want to reinforce. Through repetition and practice, parallel revision solidifies students' metacognitive understanding of and ability to deploy the rhetorical moves needed to adjust their communicative meaning in English sentences for varied audiences and purposes.

Design and Implementation Tips

We've said it before, but we will say it again: it's harder to create a strong stretch strategy than it looks; but since they do so many things at once (developing content, strong writing, reading comprehension, academic vocabulary and the foundations of academic literacy), it's well worth the time it takes. Work with a colleague or two to identify essential content and then play with the activities as you design them, always sitting in the seat of your imagined students and writing what you think they would write when given your activity. Based on what emerges, redesign your task, fiddling with what you actually provide (in the stem or the sentences) versus what you are hoping for the students to provide. Be intentional about the level of sentence complexity you are expecting from your students, starting small and building the level of challenge gradually.

Note that stretch activities, like all those in Combinations, can and should be differentiated to meet the varied levels of English language proficiency for your students. For example, any of the stretch strategies can be provided in a receptive (rather than productive) form, as in the expansion example in Figure 6.7, where students are asked to consider and discuss orally what makes a particular expanded sentence better than the original.

Home language can and should be drawn upon flexibly to support your instructional goals, with the one caveat that students should not write combined sentences in home language, since the purpose here is to teach English syntax. In expansion, teachers should make sure students understand the kernel if it is written in English. This can be done in various ways, including by providing a verbal explanation or written translation. A teacher could also show students annotations of the words in the kernel.

Directions: Below you will find simple and expanded sentences drawn from our reading of *How Sugar Changed the World.*

Read the simple and the expanded sentences.

Annotate the expanded sentence for what information it provides (who, what, when, where, why or how).

Discuss with a partner. What made the expanded sentence an improvement?

Simple sentence: They used it to show off.

              Who?   What?   Where?

Expanded sentence <u>Affluent Muslims</u> used <u>sugar</u> <u>in edible sculptures and extravagant displays</u> to

    Why?
<u>show off their wealth and generosity.</u>

Explain what makes the expanded sentence an improvement:
_____
_____

FIGURE 6.7 Example of using stretch strategies provided in a receptive (rather than productive form), where students are asked to consider and discuss orally what makes a particular expanded sentence better than the original.

A student is provided the kernel in home language and answers the question words in home language. The expanded sentence is written in English.

A ella no le gusta Spider.

Quien? ....

Porque?...

Expanded Sentence: Lupe does not like Spider because he is in a gang.

A student may do the task entirely in English, and then, translate the expanded sentence into their home language.

She does not like Spider.
Who? ....
Why?...
Expanded Sentence: Lupe does not like Spider because he is in a gang.
Translation: A Lupe no le gusta Spider porque está en una pandilla.

FIGURE 6.8 Example of a student writing notes in their home language and writing the expanded sentence in English.

Students can jot down notes for the question words in their home language instead of English, which will help them to clarify their thinking first. After expanding the sentence in English, the student can translate the expanded sentence back into the home language (Garcia & Menken, 2015), as seen in Figure 6.8.

A teacher implementing stretch strategies can do so using various methods of quality instruction for multilingual learners. The importance of modeling, for instance, cannot be overstated. For all of these strategies, teachers should model and think aloud to allow students to watch the teacher make syntactic choices in the service of clear expressions of meaning. As the teacher models, they should emphasize the function of the choices (e.g., "Here I am adding the *what*"). Students will then learn to appropriate these syntactic choices and incorporate them into their own linguistic practices through repeated exposure. As students' English proficiency grows, they will have a better understanding of how language works in English to implement these moves on their own.

The following vignette shows a teacher, Ms. Karina Akter, using the expansion strategy in support of her content and language objectives and illustrates how all of what we hope for (high-level content, analytical thinking and developing linguistic complexity) can be worked on all at once even for students who are new to English. Notice in particular how the teacher explicitly breaks down step by step how to incorporate rich detail into the sentence and helps students keep track of the underlying skeleton of the sentence and how to think meaningfully about the content while she models for students how to expand the sentence to incorporate those ideas. The modeling here from the teacher is critical to make it visible for students to see transparently each step along the way. Notice also the opportunities for students to collaborate and use social interaction to engage in problem-solving.

> **VIGNETTE A   Stretch It Out: A Vignette with Sentence Expansion**
>
> Ms. Karina Akter is teaching a ninth-grade ELA course using standard-aligned instructional materials. Instead of simplifying her curricula for her students, who are mostly new to learning English, she has decided to hone in on the students' content knowledge by utilizing sentence expansion alongside their reading of the Langston Hughes poem *I, Too*.
>
> After introducing the stretch strategy a few times using familiar content, Ms. Akter feels her students are ready to expand sentences on their own, but she wants to focus on modeling an example from beginning to end to make sure they really understand the strategy. When assessing the students previously, she saw they had a grasp of the poem's meaning; she now wants to see how they can express their understanding in English of what they learned about the author's perspective in the poem.
>
> Ms. Akter says to her students, "Today we will use what we learned about the poem *I, Too* to expand a sentence kernel". She displays and reads aloud a simple sentence written on the board:
>
> He feels proud.
>
> "Students, when someone feels proud, it means they feel good about who they are and what they have done. How

might you say 'proud' in your language?" Ms. Akter asks some of her more English-proficient students to translate "proud" into different languages so that other newcomers can understand.

Ms. Akter asks the students, "Can you think of an example when you felt 'proud'?" Many students raise their hands excitedly, so Ms. Akter asks the students to turn to tell a partner about their example. As they discuss, Ms. Akter listens in and provides another explanation when she hears one student who does not quite understand the meaning.

"I want you to think about how the author of *I, Too* feels proud when you expand this sentence kernel". Ms. Akter asks the class to read the kernel aloud together. She shows the students the whole task with the question words.

He feels proud.
  Who?……………………..
  When?……………………
  Why?……………………

"Now this is a very simple sentence", she says, reading and pointing to the kernel. "And it doesn't tell us a lot of information. Let's think about each question word and see how we can add new interesting facts and detail to make it a great sentence about the poem".

Ms. Akter re-reads the kernel. Then she circles "he" and annotates it with "who?" and asks the class, "Who is the 'he' in the poem? Write down your notes on the dotted line". She sees most students write down "poet" or "Langston Hughes" on the dotted line.

"I see you are all thinking what I am thinking! The 'he' is talking about the poet, Langston Hughes". She writes down her notes (Langston Hughes) on the dotted line next to the question word on the board.

Ms. Akter reads the kernel again. "Now we need to expand the sentence with *when*. When does the poet feel proud? You may need to go back to the poem to find the answer. I'll give you some time to talk with your partner and I want you to add notes on the dotted line next to the *when* after you both decide the answer".

Ms. Akter listens in as students collaborate with partners. She sees them reference the poem. A few students are explaining it to each other in their home language. "Class, I see a few different excellent answers for the *when* in the sentence". Ms. Akter elicits a few possibilities from students and charts them on the board. Then she asks the class which answer they should use. The class picks one (when company comes to visit) and she inserts that in the notes section on the board.

Then Ms. Akter says: "Let's think about where in the sentence could we put this information. Could we do it here [pointing] at the beginning of the sentence? Or could we add to the kernel at the end [pointing]? This is a choice we need to make! Raise your hand if you think we should do it at the beginning of the sentence. [Students raise their hand.] Raise your hand if you think we should do it at the end of the sentence. [Students raise their hand.] Thank you for your vote! We could do it either way. I will choose to do it at the beginning of the sentence!"

Ms. Akter expands the kernel on the board as students observe.

When company comes to visit, the poet feels proud.

Ms. Akter reads the kernel again. "Wow! Our sentence is getting clearer! We have more detail now. Are we done? Do we have all the facts we need? I don't feel we have enough. What do you think?"

One student says he thinks it's enough. Another agrees.

Ms. Akter continues, "It could be enough. But I think we could add some more information. What is another question we could ask that would get us even more detail?" She points to an anchor chart that lists all the question words in English and is translated into five different languages. "Another question that will really make this sentence pop is *why*. I want you to think about why the poet feels proud. Talk to your partner and write it in your notes next to the question word 'why.'"

Ms. Akter walks around the class and listens to students. She asks more proficient students to help her translate for newcomers. She refers students to look back at the text they were reading and their notes.

Ms. Akter brings the class back together and writes a few ideas in the notes next to the question word on the board. "I heard you all say that the poet was proud because he is strong and beautiful". She points to her notes and points to the question word "why".

"Now class, watch me as I use all your wonderful ideas to build an awesome sentence". She writes the expanded sentence and points to the question word and the notes each time she expands with a detail so that students can see the correlation between the notes and the expanded sentence.

When company comes to visit, the poet feels proud because he knows he is strong and beautiful.

She reads the sentence aloud. As she reads it, she scoops the sentence into sections and points back to the original kernel and to the notes to show how the details were incorporated into the syntax of the sentence to expand its meaning and detail. Ms. Akter narrates for her students the choices needed to construct the expanded sentence using the notes and details.

She puts up her annotated example on the wall so that students can refer to and remember the process that was used to expand the sentence. In future lessons, she refers back to her annotated example to remind students as they continue practicing with new expansion tasks.

Closing

Combinations presents a real shift in the classroom. Most educators would not imagine a lesson in which language and ideas are deconstructed in such specific ways, and some may balk at the amount of time it might take to engage students in the strategies. However, in varying and gradual ways, the stretch strategies we present teach students to become cognizant of the linguistic moves through which complexity is built at the sentence level. In learning to produce more complex expressions of academic meaning within sentences, students also become able to deduce complexity when they read within and across sentences. Through repeated practice, the linguistic moves used to generate complexity become internalized by students; thus they become able to understand and express a world of nuance and precision in academic content which was previously not available to them in English.

References

Abutaleb, Y. (2022, August 22). Fauci plans to step down in December after half a century in government. *Washington Post*. https://www.washingtonpost.com/health/2022/08/22/fauci-retiring/

Garcia, O., & Menken, L. (2015). Cultivating an ecology of multilingualism in schools. In B. Spolsky, O. Inbar-Lourie, & M. Tannenbaum (Eds.), *Challenges for language education and policy: Making-space for people*. Routledge. https://doi.org/10.4324/9781315884288

Graham, S., & Perin, D. (2007). Writing next: Effective strategies to improve writing of adolescents in middle and high schools – A report to Carnegie corporation of New York. *Alliance for Excellent Education*. https://media.carnegie.org/filer_public/3c/f5/3cf58727-34f4-4140-a014-723a00ac56f7/ccny_report_2007_writing.pdf

Hebert, M., Kearns, D. M., Hayes, J. B., Bazis, P., & Cooper, S. (2018). Why children with dyslexia struggle with writing and how to help them. *Language, Speech, and Hearing Services in Schools*, 49(4), 843–863.

Saddler, B. (2012). *Teacher's guide to effective sentence writing.* Guilford Press.

Scott, C. M. (2009). A case for the sentence in reading comprehension. *Language, Speech and Hearing Services in Schools, 40,* 184–191. https://doi.org/10.1044/0161-1461(2008/08-0042)

7

Design and Teaching Tips

Multilingual Entry Points for Combinations

What Are Multilingual Entry Points for Combinations?

In earlier chapters, we make the case that Combinations is effective for supporting the development of academic literacy in English across a range of learner characteristics, experiences and needs, and we provide some examples of how Combinations can and should be adapted for different students. In this chapter, we dig into multilingual entry points more deeply. These entry points are the adjustments teachers can and should make in both design and implementation to ensure that Combinations fulfills its potential for all students. Some entry points are temporary scaffolds for those who need them. Others are best practices for the teaching of Combinations to all multilingual learners, and in fact to all students. Overall, the entry points make Combinations and content broadly accessible through multiple means of engagement, representation and expression (CAST, 2018).

Our toolkit of entry points, aligned with research on high-quality instruction for multilingual learners but not by any means a comprehensive list of all the ways to scaffold literacy instruction for any student population, includes:

For designing Combinations:

1. Use receptive tasks to scaffold expressive language development
2. Make language accessible and comprehensible
3. Develop vocabulary knowledge

For implementing Combinations:

4. Model with examples and explicit instruction
5. Integrate social interaction and discussion
6. Use all language modalities

For designing and implementing Combinations:

7. Use home language as a critical tool for learning and thinking
8. Promote metalinguistic awareness and cross-linguistic connections
9. Use Combinations in oral language

Many, though not all students, will need the entry points to engage fully in the linguistic problem-solving called for in Combinations. Students may benefit from these entry points especially if they are newcomers, have learning differences, experienced interrupted schooling, have language-based disabilities or are dual-identified as multilingual learners with a learning disability, and/or struggle with executive functioning challenges.

In this chapter, we aim to show a more detailed portrait than was possible earlier about what each entry point includes and how it fits with and supports literacy and content learning in English through Combinations. By highlighting and amplifying the thinking and language processing involved in more broken-down, concrete and discrete moves, we show how these entry points build understanding and fluency for any student needing additional support than is provided within a generic Combinations task with literacy.

Again, ours is not an exhaustive list of entry points; we know that you will draw upon and discover more of your own. We present those we have found to be most practical, widely applicable and powerful for amplifying learning through Combinations. In this chapter, we also hope to show how Combinations, in being so adaptable via integration with the entry points, provides a powerful vehicle for bringing research-based best practices into the classroom to allow access for all students.

The Entry Points

While we number and describe each entry point separately for clarity, in practice, a teacher will draw upon them flexibly (not in a set order) and often in concert with one another rather than one at a time as needed by their students.

Entry Points Related to Task Design

Entry Point Number 1: Use Receptive Tasks to Scaffold Expressive Language Development
Considering where students fall on an English language and literacy development continuum, you may temporarily provide students opportunities to use receptive language skills (reading and listening) rather than productive ones (writing and speaking) to engage in the language structures and content in less linguistically demanding ways. If students are not yet developmentally ready to produce the ideas at hand in English, receptive tasks provide students with support to first notice and observe how language is used and then be able to transfer that knowledge to produce the language on their own.

For example, for a student who may not quite be ready to produce all of the English language required in an expansion task embedded in content, a teacher could design a task that reinforces and assesses knowledge of the same content and language structures while requiring less language production, as in the example in Figure 6.7 in Chapter 6. Note that the teacher's task is in bold and the anticipated student responses are in italics.

In Figure 6.7, students engage with sophisticated language and content in a receptive fashion. They are noticing *how* and *where* (the syntax) language and ideas were added in order to expand and improve the sentence kernel. The productive requirements of this activity – what students are actually expected to produce in written form – are less than what will be expected when their expressive language skills in English are more developed. Students will be asked to produce more of the content-based language independently after they have seen a few examples and engaged in it through reading and observation.

Entry Point Number 2: Make Tasks Accessible and Comprehensible to Students

Combinations strategies should use content and language that is comprehensible, in other words, that students are already familiar with or learning about (Krashen, 2003). If you use words and phrases that are not yet familiar to students to align with your content objectives, be intentional about how you make the tasks accessible through the use of home language (see entry point number 7), nonlinguistic supports, and/or by breaking down the task into smaller steps.

Visuals or images that are paired with the tasks provide relevant background information that students can use to access the task and consider the conceptual relationships they need to express in the sentence completions. They provide a nonlinguistic way to help students generate ideas and language. In your instruction, guide students to use the image or visual as they engage in problem-solving and thinking about the sentence they need to create.

Breaking down tasks into smaller pieces is critical for some students. In a *because, but & so* task, for example, a particular student could begin just with *because*. In *expansion*, a student could be asked at first to answer just one or two questions. In Figure 7.1, for example, students are asked to expand by answering only the questions "why" and "how". Note that the design of this task draws upon multiple entry points simultaneously: visuals and

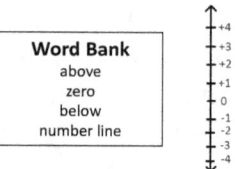

Directions: Use the word bank and the picture to expand the simple sentences below.

Simple sentence: I know -3 is a negative number.

    Why? _because it is below zero on the number line_

    Where? _on the number line_

Expanded sentence: _I know -3 is a negative number because it is below zero on the number line._

FIGURE 7.1 Example of students expanding answers using "why" and "how".

breaking down a task (entry point number 2) and a word bank (see entry point number 3).

Entry Point Number 3: Develop Vocabulary Knowledge

Developing vocabulary as students build content knowledge is particularly beneficial for students' overall language and literacy growth (Graves, et al., 2012; Kieffer & Lesaux, 2007). Combinations is highly effective in building knowledge and vocabulary within tasks that simultaneously ask students to consider how language works.

As students engage in linguistic problem-solving with Combinations, many will benefit from being provided with a word bank to help them complete their sentences (See Figure 7.1). The word bank should include pre-taught or pre-identified words within a unit of study. The students can use these words to construct their new sentences. Word banks can include words that are conceptually related to the core idea of the Combinations task. This supports students in establishing the existing relationship between ideas and focusing their energy on pulling together the language needed to express that relationship in a constructed sentence.

Entry Points Related to Implementation

Entry Point Number 4: Model Combinations with Examples and Explicit Instruction

As with all learning objectives, all students (and especially those new to learning English) need to see models of each strategy being completed. All students benefit from multiple exposures before they can engage in the strategy independently (Hollingsworth & Ybarra, 2012). In addition to showing how the task itself operates, the goal of modeling in Combinations is for the teacher to make thinking about language visible to students, to demystify the choices made as one goes through a task, so that students can see the decision-making process when they engage in linguistic problem-solving on their own. (As an example, see the Vignette for Sentence Expansion in Chapter 5, where a teacher models how to do a sentence expansion.) Through repeated modeling, students learn how to make syntactic choices on their own. Ideally, teachers would model Combinations tasks using their home language for newcomers, making their thinking and decisions visible in the language students are most familiar with.

For example, a teacher can model with mentor sentences that show how to use each of the conjunctions for *hook it up* and *set it up* strategies, using content that is already familiar to students. This could be content from a previous lesson that students know, so that they are not spending their mental energy focusing on the meaning but on the function and meaning of the unfamiliar conjunction.

For example, the teacher might show students the following completed mentor sentences:

- Actors must rehearse **because** they need to make characters come alive.
- Actors must rehearse, **but** at times they improvise.
- Actors must rehearse, **so** they spend many hours practicing their lines.

When the teacher provides these mentor sentences, they can do a think-aloud about the relationships in the examples – using *because* to name a reason for why actors need to rehearse, using *but* to name a different idea other than rehearsal and using *so* to name the result of having to rehearse.

As students become familiar with the linguistic structures in a Combinations strategy, teachers should also model *how the language works in the particular context of that strategy*. For example, when learning the appositive strategy, it is common for students learning English to insert a phrase that is correct in its meaning but may not be grammatically correct, as in the following:

> Thomas Jefferson, he was the third President, helped write the Declaration of Independence.

The teacher can model how to express the same idea within one sentence using an appositive, as follows:

> Thomas Jefferson, the third President of the United States, helped write the Declaration of Independence.

In modeling, the teacher would point out explicitly to students that the sentences both have the same meaning, but that one uses the appositive structure. We want students to understand that the same idea and meaning can be communicated correctly in varied ways, such as with an adverbial phrase (Thomas Jefferson, who was the third President…), and that using the appositive is one choice a writer makes for style and emphasis.

Teachers can also model the process of how to arrange word order and syntax when combining sentences. Students can observe how their teacher moves words around to combine given sentences. A ceramics teacher, for example, might provide these two sentences and ask students to combine them.

> Pinch is a hand building pottery technique.
> Coil is a hand building pottery technique.

This teacher might model through a think-aloud and verbalize their decision-making to make thinking visible to students. The teacher can point out the redundant parts of the sentences. They can point out the need for "and" to join the two items, *pinch* and *coil*. The teacher can point to and annotate the given sentences as they think-aloud, and then, write out the combined sentence for students to see, as follows:

> Combined sentence: Pinch and coil are hand building pottery techniques.

As students' English proficiency grows, they will have a better understanding of how language works to do this on their own. Teachers can accelerate their understanding by "pulling back the curtains" to show students what happens behind the scenes in sentence construction.

Entry Point Number 5: Integrate Social Interaction and Discussion with Combinations

Multilingual learners will benefit from working collaboratively with peers and explaining their thinking in English and in home language as they problem-solve to complete a Combinations task. Through social interaction, students' thinking about content and language is made visible and audible to peers; academic discourse is where the learning magic happens (Zwiers & Crawford, 2011).

Discussing ideas students see in the written tasks and then applying the rules of syntax to complete Combinations tasks in writing supports students to play with language. It asks them to consider how word order and word choice are used to effectively communicate the relationships they are thinking about. Discussion and interaction set the linguistic foundation for students to nail down and effectively communicate their ideas in written form.

Consider the example we mentioned in Figure 6.7 about how sugar was used in different cultures. The students need to expand the kernel (They used it to show off) using four different question words. Perhaps students in a group are each assigned one of the question words (either who, what, where or why) to expand the kernel in one way. Then one student would share the *who*, another would share the *what*, etc. Together, they would construct the newly expanded sentence collaboratively. This might require some negotiating to determine the accuracy of the information provided by each student, and the word order. They might point out different reasons why sugar was considered a status symbol, resulting in a variety of expanded sentences all based on the same original kernel. Alternatively, students might work on an expansion individually and then read their expanded sentences aloud to each other, using them in a discussion about the importance of sugar in history.

With the appositive strategy, a student might, for example, verbally generate phrases that can be used as an appositive, before writing one down in the sentence frame. Let's say the sentence frame provided was:

The Declaration of Independence, _____, officially established the United States.

Students could first work in pairs or groups to discuss possible ways to define the Declaration of Independence based on what they have studied. They might use their home language to discuss this as well. Students can then work with peers to then insert an appositive in English in written form they feel best represents their understanding. The students might list a number of possibilities like those below and discuss together which one they ultimately think should be used to complete the sentence:

- a document adopted on July 4, 1776
- a historical document from Congress
- an act of rebellion against British rule

These kinds of opportunities for discussion help students to appropriate the linguistic structures and conceptual understandings within the Combinations tasks.

Entry Point Number 6: Use All Modalities of Language with Combinations

Multilingual learners need to engage in developing academic literacy through all language modalities – speaking, listening, reading and writing. As we outlined in Chapter 1, Combinations advances academic literacy in English by developing the overlapping meaning-based skills that undergird skilled reading and writing and that draw upon and span the different language modalities. Students need a strong foundation in oral language in order to develop reading and writing, and vice versa, in a new language; the different modalities reinforce and mutually strengthen one another (Gibbons, 2014). Implementing Combinations to reinforce the reciprocal development of speech and print skills is especially beneficial for multilingual learners because it develops multiple aspects of academic literacy in integrated and content-based ways.

To reinforce the development of *reading*, Combinations tasks can be designed to be text-dependent, so that students are required to return to and use information from a text they are reading to construct a sentence. For example, the teacher can indicate specific parts of a text from which students should draw information to expand a sentence kernel or to complete a sentence stem that begins with a subordinating conjunction.

To reinforce the development of *speaking* and *listening*, teachers should provide opportunities for students to *say* and *listen* to each other's sentences after they have written them. After completing sentences individually, for example, students could pair up to hear each other's sentences and give each other feedback on meaning, fluency and accuracy. After combining a set of given sentences, students could read the sentences aloud to practice fluency. After unscrambling a sentence, they might read it aloud to check if they are right. By saying and hearing the sentences created using Combinations, students begin to appropriate the linguistic structures in written form into their oral language. When students can hear and say the sentence patterns in Combinations, they will notice and observe that what they *say* can be encoded and imprinted in written expression, helping them see the correlation between what is in their oral language with what is written in print.

Entry Points Used for Both Design and Implementation

Entry Point Number 7: Use Home Language as a Critical Tool for Learning and Thinking

Home language should be incorporated to support students' thinking about and expression of academic ideas (García & Menken, 2015). Home language can be used to support students' comprehension of and access to the Combinations tasks. It can also be used to support students' solutions for (or completion of) the strategies. When using home language with Combinations, be strategic about when and how students use their home language to support the learning objectives.

Complete the following sentences.

美國民主自由正受到威脅因為。。。
美國民主自由正受到威脅，但是。。。
美國民主自由正受到威脅，所以。。。

Glossary

因為 because   但是 but   所以 so

美國 America   民主 democracy   威脅 threat

FIGURE 7.2 Example of providing a Combinations strategy entirely in the home language.

For example, when first introducing a Combinations strategy, it may be appropriate to provide it for the first time entirely in the home language (if and when this is possible). See Figure 7.2. In this example, a glossary is provided so those who cannot read Chinese can see how this translation of a *because, but & so* strategy looks in a different language.

When a Combinations task is provided in English, students can annotate the task in their home language for any English words they do not yet recognize. For example, students might annotate the sentence stems in their home language before they complete them, so that they understand the nature of the relationship they need to articulate. Students might annotate in their home language the sentence frame with the appositive strategy, or the kernel with the sentence expansion strategy, to ascertain its meaning and then determine what appositive to insert. The purpose is to make sure that the language in the Combinations tasks is comprehensible to students, so that students can make sense of the linguistic task they are trying to solve.

Once students understand the purpose of the Combinations strategy, it is not necessary to provide a translation of the Combinations task when the goal is English language development. This encourages productive struggle with the linguistic problem at hand in English. Instead, provide a question in their home language that prompts students to think about the topic and relationship that is needed to complete the task. This creates an opportunity for students to work toward resolution as they consider the meaning of the stem in English. You may translate components of the task that students need in order to access the task. For example, students may need direct translation of the conjunctions with similar meanings or functions that are used in their home language (*but* in English is *pero* in Spanish and 可是 in Chinese). Multilingual learners will benefit from knowing the equivalent word or phrase used in their language with the function of communicating the same relationship.

For the most part, students should have the freedom to use their home language to respond to a Combinations task. Students should discuss the conceptual relationships in the task in their home language and should be free to complete a sentence stem in their home language. They may also choose to draft ideas in their home language before writing the sentence(s) in English. However, consider the situations in which using the home language may reduce the potency of the Combinations tasks when literacy development in English is the instructional goal. For example, student responses still need to ultimately be constructed in English when it comes to sentence sorts, scrambles and sentence combining since the tasks require working directly with English syntax. In these cases, it is not effective or possible to ask students to complete the task in their home language. The point is to give students opportunities to work with the given sentences in English and figure out the syntactic choices they can make to solve the problem. However, it may be beneficial for multilingual learners to talk in their home language as they process their thinking and approach to solving the problem.

Be strategic in your instructions for which language students should use to complete a Combinations task. For example, students can jot down notes for the question words in their home language instead of English for sentence expansion, which will help them clarify their thinking first. They can construct the expanded sentence in English. The student can then translate the expanded sentence back into their home language. This ratchets up the rigor needed in thinking and linguistic decision-making. See Figure 6.8 in Chapter 6 for an example.

Entry Point Number 8: Promote Metalinguistic Awareness and Cross-Linguistic Connections

Teachers should create explicit opportunities for students to notice how language works and how they use language as a way to deepen students' awareness of language practices (Achugar et al., 2007). Doing so also deepens students' thinking about the content and promotes understanding and the transfer of understanding and skills across languages. The goal is to create conditions where students are actively discussing their linguistic problem-solving together – what did they do with language, what choices did they make? This will solidify their understanding of how language works to express academic ideas in English.

Combinations offers routines that directly connect to content-based meaning that encourage such metalinguistic and cross-linguistic conversations. For example, students might notice and discuss the ways in which the conjunctions are used to establish different meanings using *hook it up* or *set it up* strategies. They might share with peers their answers to questions such as: what is the difference in meaning in this sentence using *because* and the sentence using *so*? When you used *but* in this sentence, what changed in your thinking? In sentence expansion, students might annotate or color-code the functions of the words and phrases in an expanded sentence that correlate with question words. The teacher could explicitly point these out to the students to reinforce their consciousness of the meaningful chunks they brought together to form the sentence.

Multilingual learners also benefit significantly from the act of translating, which requires the students to carefully consider the language being used and the ideas to be expressed. The process of translating builds students' cross-linguistic awareness and a better understanding of the language structures in English. Requiring student translations of the sentences they produce in Combinations (as opposed to providing a translation) can support cross-linguistic comparison.

For example, with Sentence Types, students might write the four sentences in English and then translate the sentences in their home language, or the other way around. This may be a needed scaffold to help students complete the task. In doing so, they may also generate new insights about the content they are learning. Students might also, for example, compare the conjunctions used in English and those used in their home language to link ideas and connect relationships in similar or different ways.

Entry Point Number 9 – Use Combinations Verbally, at First

If students are not yet able to engage in Combinations in written form for various reasons (i.e., young children just learning letter–sound correspondence, newcomers with no previous exposure to the English language, or students whose home languages are not commonly used in written form), they will benefit from engaging with modified Combinations tasks orally. Teachers can build a strong academic literacy foundation in oral language. Doing so allows multilingual learners to engage with complex academic thinking and vocabulary even before they are ready to read or write about the academic concepts being studied on their own.

Consider, for example, the second- and third-grade students in the Literacy Academy Collective's two pilot classrooms for students with language-based disabilities at PS 161 in the Bronx, led by Ilia Edwards.[1] These students, some of whom were multilingual learners, had missed two critical years of consistent in-school instruction due to COVID-19. Many came to their first year in the program not yet able to decode words or to write letters. While their teachers – Jennifer Baron, Nicholena Lovett and Liz McQuestion on the second-grade team and Vanessa Anderson, Mara Ast and Rachel Frias on the third-grade team – focused a large part of their efforts on teaching their students to read and to write letters and words, they also provided instruction in grade-level, standard-based academic content. They found that using Combinations tasks in oral language supported students' critical thinking and sophisticated expression about the academic content while laying a foundation for academic writing.

To move all of their students' critical thinking and verbal expression forward in spite of the fact that many could not yet

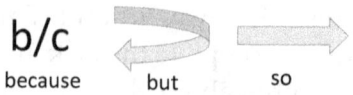

FIGURE 7.3 Example of symbols representing because, but and so.

produce written sentences about academic content, for example, they utilized the *because, but* & *so* strategy in oral language. They created laminated cards with symbols representing each conjunction on the front and the written-out meaning of the conjunction on the back. First, they taught students to memorize the symbols for each conjunction, as seen in Figure 7.3.

Then, after modeling what they expected and practicing with familiar vocabulary, they moved the activity into academic content. They asked students to hold these cards in their hands, selecting and holding up the card with the specific conjunction they were using when they talked (sometimes in pairs, sometimes individually at the front of the room or at their desks) in oral sentences about the content and utilizing the academic vocabulary they were learning. During the second-grade unit on communities, Leo held up the "b/c" symbol and said: "Urban life is exciting because there is many fun things to do". During the third grade unit on Mexican Holidays, one student who was new to English and the United States held up her symbol for but and said, "People dress up as skeletons on the Day of the Dead, but it's not scary". (See Figure 7.4).

Note that in these examples, the stems (Urban life is exciting because… and People dress up as skeletons on the Day of the Dead…) were provided verbally by the teacher. The students repeated this stem verbally as they expressed an entire sentence.

People dress up as skeletons on the Day of the Dead <u>*because they are celebrating their relatives who have died*</u>.
People dress up as skeletons on the Day of the Dead, but <u>*it's not scary*</u>.
People dress up as skeletons on the Day of the Dead, <u>*so you should too*</u>!

FIGURE 7.4 Student responses about Mexican holidays.

FIGURE 7.5 Example of student calaveras drawing (skeleton drawing).
Photo courtesy of Logan.

Note as well that symbols require little language to represent complex relationships. Therefore, they work wonderfully to prompt complexity in oral language. Another benefit is that these symbols can also be used in students' note-taking in the future.

In a progressive task moving from purely oral language to some written language, the third-grade teachers asked the students to draw their own calaveras (skeleton drawings) and to explain why theirs was silly rather than scary using *because, but & so*. Again, the teachers provided sentence stems that students were asked to complete. This time, however, students produced written responses to the extent that they were able. In this way, the teachers worked to solidify the speech-to-print connection. Logan drew a calaveras riding a skateboard (Figure 7.5) and completed each sentence stem – read aloud by the teacher – on his own orally. Then, with teacher support, he wrote his answer to complete the first sentence stem using *because*. His completions for the second and third stems using *but* and *so* were scribed by the teacher (See Figure 7.6).

"Something I noticed", Ilia said in reflecting on the impact of this work, "is that once we taught students *because, but & so* [in oral language], the opportunities to practice were everywhere! – when talking about a read aloud, on a field trip, in a social situation. Language begets more language!"

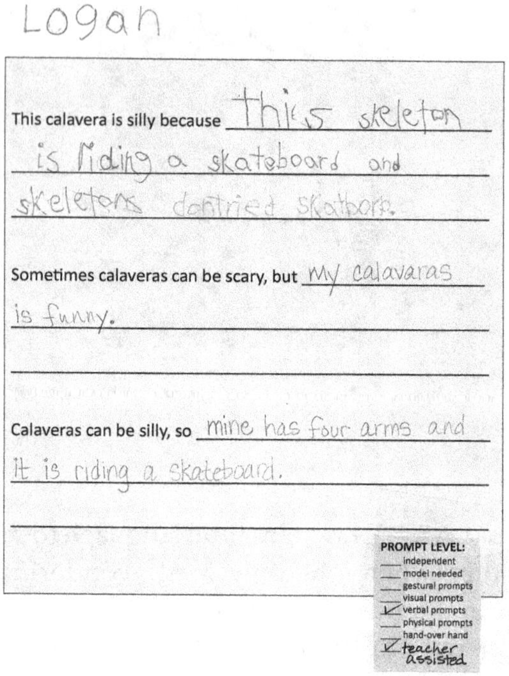

> Logan
>
> This calavera is silly because **this skeleton is riding a skateboard and skeletons dontried skatbors.**
>
> Sometimes calaveras can be scary, but **My calavaras is funny.**
>
> Calaveras can be silly, so **mine has four arms and it is riding a skateboard.**
>
> PROMPT LEVEL:
> ___ independent
> ___ model needed
> ___ gestural prompts
> ___ visual prompts
> ✓ verbal prompts
> ___ physical prompts
> ___ hand-over hand
> ✓ teacher assisted

FIGURE 7.6 Example of student using the prompts of because, but and so to explain why their calveras (skeleton drawing) was silly.

Photo courtesy of Logan.

The Language Development Continuum – One Way to Conceptualize Entry Points

One way in which teachers may conceptualize and use multilingual entry points is to support students on various points along the language development continuum. State and district school systems in the United States use a variety of frameworks to describe English language development and proficiency levels used for assessment purposes (e.g., the WIDA English Language Development Standards Framework (2020), The ELPA21 Assessment System or the New York State English as a Second Language Achievement Test). In general, these language frameworks progress from emerging language skills in English toward increasing comprehension of linguistic input, increasing linguistic output in both speaking and writing modalities, increasing vocabulary and increasing syntactic complexity.

Conceptualizing the range of possible entry points in terms of how they map across a language continuum can be a useful starting point. Consider the example in Figure 7.7 which illustrates how students across the continuum of language development could engage with the same sentence-level task and content. Note that the task itself (identifying and repairing fragments) and the thinking involved are not simplified. Rather, students are provided with different ways to engage with the skill and content according to their level of English language proficiency.

Specifically note how small adjustments made by drawing upon various entry points provide access to students at varying points across the continuum:

- At the *Entering* level, students may not yet understand enough about English syntax to repair a fragment. They still need to develop an understanding of word order, so a cloze exercise that uses the same underlying sentence skeleton may be most appropriate.
- At the *Emerging* level, students are ready to make more linguistic choices and can complete (repair) the sentence more independently. Note that in Figure 7.7, they are still provided with an academic vocabulary word to use in their response.
- At the *Transitioning* level, the linguistic demands are greater because there isn't just one way to repair the fragment. There are several linguistic choices students can make. Notice that the underlying sentence skeleton (and therefore the content and thinking) is the same as the tasks designed for other levels of language proficiency.
- At the *Expanding* level, the goal is to pull for more sophisticated and precise use of vocabulary with the same underlying sentence skeleton (same content and thinking).

We understand that a teacher will not necessarily have time to create a differentiated task for every student each day, and our purpose in showing the examples in Figure 7.7 is not to recommend that teachers do so! Rather, we want to illustrate how entry points can target students' level of language development across a continuum.

Level 1 Entering	Level 2 Emerging	Level 3 Transitioning	Level 4 Commanding/Expanding
✓ Provide visual ✓ Make cloze ✓ Provide word bank	✓ Provide visual ✓ Provide sentence frame ✓ Provide vocabulary word	✓ Provide visual ✓ ~~Provide cloze or sentence frame~~ ✓ Provide word bank	✓ ~~Provide picture~~ ✓ ~~Provide cloze or sentence frame~~ ✓ ~~Provide word bank~~ ✓ Provide glossary
Select words from the word bank to fill in the blanks Word bank: A, An, equal, unequal ___ isosceles triangle has ___ sides.	Use the provided vocabulary word to complete the sentence frame. Word: equal An isosceles triangle has ___	Repair fragment by using the words in the word bank. Word bank: equal, length an isosceles triangle ___	Repair fragment by using at least one of the words in the glossary. **congruent**: identical in form (equal) **altitude**–a line segment through a vertex and perpendicular to (i.e., forming a right angle with) a line containing the base (the side opposite the vertex) an isosceles triangle ___

FIGURE 7.7 Example of different ways to engage the skill and content according to students level of English language proficiency.

Closing

As you design Combinations tasks, sit in the seats of different students in your class to determine which entry points, or compilation of entry points, are most needed at a particular moment in time. You should draw flexibly from our toolkit of entry points, adding some of your own, to support your specific students. And as you collect and make sense of your students' responses, you will continuously adjust your design and implementation of entry points over time.

The multilingual entry points ensure that all students, especially those who are finding it hardest to access grade-level content through conventional teaching methods, can participate in the learning, thinking and development of academic literacy provided by Combinations. With the entry points, differentiated Combinations tasks and scaffolds still hew closely to the core content objectives that all students are learning. Over time, the Combinations strategies accelerate students learning, academic thinking and literacy in English so that those same students are able to achieve academic success.

Note

1 These classrooms, a 2022–2023 pilot for a new public school for students with dyslexia opening in Fall 2023, formed part of Mayor Eric Adams plan to address the literacy crisis in New York City schools with a particular focus on serving students with dyslexia (see Fadulu, 2022).

References

Achugar, M., Schleppegrell, M., & Oteíza, T. (2007). Engaging teachers in language analysis: A functional linguistics approach to reflective literacy. *English teaching: Practice and critique, 6*(2), 8–24. https://files.eric.ed.gov/fulltext/EJ832185.pdf

CAST (2018). Universal Design for Learning Guidelines version 2.2. *UDL Guidelines*. http://udlguidelines.cast.org

Fadulu, L. (2022, May 12). Mayor Adams unveils program to address dyslexia in N.Y.C. schools. *The New York Times*. https://www.nytimes.com/2022/05/12/nyregion/adams-dyslexia-nyc-schools.html

García, O., & Menken, K. (2015). Cultivating an ecology of multilingualism in schools. In B. Spolsky, O. Inbar-Lourie, & M. Tannenbaum (Eds.), *Challenges for language education and policy: Making space for people*. Routledge.

Gibbons, P. (2014). *Scaffolding language, scaffolding learning: Teaching English language learners in the mainstream classroom* (2nd ed). Heinemann.

Graves, M. F., August, D., & Mancilla-Martinez, J. (2012). *Teaching vocabulary to English language learners*. Teachers College Press.

Hollingsworth, J. R., & Ybarra, S. E. (2012). *Explicit direct instruction for English learners*. Corwin Press.

Kieffer, M. J., & Lesaux, N. K. (2007). Breaking down words to build meaning: Morphology, vocabulary, and reading comprehension in the urban classroom. *The Reading Teacher*, *61*(2), 134–144.

Krashen, S. (2003). *Explorations in language acquisition and Use: The Taipei lectures*. Heinemann.

Zwiers, J., & Crawford, M. (2011). *Academic conversations: Classroom talk that fosters critical thinking and content understandings*. Stenhouse Publishers.

Part III

What It Looks Like on the Ground

8

A Case Study (The Nitty Gritty of the What, How and to What Effect)

In Part I of this book, we explain Combinations and Strategic Inquiry (SI) and how together they fill a gap in the current approach to developing academic literacy for multilingual learners. In Part II, we take a deep dive into Combinations, explaining how the strategies are designed, implemented and adapted for a range of learners as well as how they support the four domains of literacy and academic content.

For clarity, in Parts I and II we organize and describe the strategies in a linear way, grouped according to their function. What may not yet be clear, as a result, is what it actually looks and feels like to engage in this work over time. In practice, Combinations is implemented in an iterative rather than a linear fashion, with teachers adjusting their selection of strategies, release of scaffolds and pacing according to evidence from ongoing inquiry into how students respond to the strategies over time.

In this chapter (the first of Part III), we present a detailed case study of one teacher's experience learning, implementing and gradually spreading Combinations plus SI in her classroom and across her school. Our purpose is to provide readers with an up close sense of *what* teachers and students are actually doing when they engage in this work along with *how* it leads to improved student performance through changes in teachers' thinking, practice and ultimately school culture. We hope to illuminate some of the granular mechanisms that undergird the larger change that we need and that our work has shown is possible.

This case focuses on the teacher's perspective and on leading change from the ground up. In the latter part of this chapter, we discuss what is possible when change from the ground up is cultivated and supported by school and district leaders with formal administrative authority. Ultimately, it is this combination of bottom-up and top down support that allows the work to thrive.

"You Were Always Smart!" Disrupting the Pathway to Long-Term English Learner Status at Mountainview

The Context and the Problem

Laura, a teacher of English Learners with ten years of experience, is in her third-year teaching at Mountainview Elementary (a pseudonym), a public school with approximately 500 students in a small city nested in mountains and farmland in New York State. For the past 20 years or so, Mountainview Elementary (Mountainview) has been changing. The population has been increasing due to a steady flow of residents fleeing more expensive and densely-packed urban areas. It is also a Sanctuary City and thus has welcomed and continues to welcome immigrant families representing many countries and languages, including Spanish, Arabic, Bengali and Vietnamese. As a result, just under 20% of the school population is now comprised of students identified as English learners, many of whom are newcomers. To date, Mountainview Elementary has hired four English as a New Language teachers to support this growing population.

Despite the welcoming stance of the city as a whole and the district's intentions, the problem – as Laura sees it – is that the reality on the ground is far from welcoming. "I've worked in other districts where ELs were not treated in this way", Laura explained. "So I was struck right away when I started working here that EL students and their teachers are just the bottom of the barrel. People see these kids as inferior". "It's not a matter of ill-will", Laura explained further.

> People want to help these kids. But they have a lot of negative assumptions. They think if ELs are in a class with general education students, that they will hold the other kids back. The teachers say things like 'I don't know what to do with those kids.' And the teachers act like they don't *need* to know.

Because of her prior experiences, Laura pushed her co-teachers as much as possible to let her have an active role in co-planning and delivering instruction. But other EL teachers did not experience the same level of collaboration. "The other three EL teachers are like teacher assistants mostly sitting in the back of the room", Laura explained. Sometimes despite her best intentions, she felt a little bit that way herself.

Perhaps not surprisingly, performance for English learners (many of them newcomers) at Mountainview was typically 15% points or more below in comparison to the performance of similar students across New York State. Even before the pandemic in 2019, it was not unusual for students at Mountainview to spend three, four or even five years in the school without budging from a beginning score of *entering* or *emerging* on the New York State English Language Assessment Test (the NYSESLAT). This test is given to students designed as English learners each year in New York State to determine their level of English language proficiency across four domains (reading, writing, speaking and listening). Students are scored in each domain and then overall as meeting one of five levels of English language proficiency: *entering, emerging, transitioning, expanding* or *commanding*, and the results are used to determine their level of English language services. English learners are expected to move up one level per year, with *entering* and *emerging* both considered beginner scores. Students who score at the *commanding* level are considered English proficient and no longer designated as English learners.

This problem of stagnating levels of English language proficiency at Mountainview (students getting stuck at the *emerging* level) was exacerbated by the COVID-19 pandemic, and students were doing much of their learning remotely. Again, Laura felt that this was not a matter of ill-will. Although teachers seemed unaware of the relationship between their negative assumptions and students' lack of progress, they did not want their students to fail. In fact, even prior to the pandemic, Mountainview had an intervention system in place to focus intensively on the students they were least successful at serving, many of whom were identified as English learners. They knew that addressing this problem was a matter of equity, and they wanted to put resources toward addressing it.

The structure they put in place was a Student Support Team (SST) to focus on the lowest performing 10% of students. A standing SST was created that included an Assistant Principal, two guidance counselors, a social worker, a reading teacher and an EL teacher. Laura was appointed as the standing EL teacher. The team focused on each student individually for one semester. Teachers who taught a particular student were invited to join a series of meetings where first the counselors would present relevant data; then invited teachers would explain "the problem" as seen from their perspective; and finally, the group would generate a list of five to eight suggestions based on what they thought the problem was. The invited teachers would pick two to three of these suggestions; implement them and gather data about student responses; and return in four six-week cycles to present evidence of impact and for the group to collectively determine the next steps.

Laura explained: "The teachers really wanted to help these kids. Sometimes they would come in almost begging for ideas about what they could do differently or better". The team brainstormed ideas, and the teachers went off eagerly to try them before returning six weeks later with the results. But, as Laura explained, these interventions never really seemed to move the needle for kids. And then, at the end of the semester, the team would say to themselves: "We tried. We did everything we could". And typically, the student would be recommended for a Special Education evaluation. It got to the point, Laura explained, where nobody really thought the SST was going to make a difference. In essence, despite everybody's best intentions, the SST had become a "gateway to special ed".

Laura felt ineffective and isolated at Mountainview. She had hoped that being on the SST would help, but was frustrated that the interventions didn't seem to be working. When she tried to talk to the general education teachers about their English learners' lack of progress, they seemed to shrug it off, acting like this was Laura's problem to solve on her own. While in theory, co-teachers were supposed to plan together, usually the general education took the lead with Laura left to figure out what her ELs needed and how to put it into instruction as an add-on. Given the urgency after the pandemic, the district adopted a new rigorous curriculum and put pressure on teachers to hold students to higher standards. Although her ELs were struggling to move beyond a beginner score, the direction from the district was to read longer and harder texts and write more but without providing any substantive support so that students could do so. "They had to read *The Wind in the Willows*! They had to write full essays! This makes no sense for my students!" Laura said.

Eager for professional learning opportunities that would help, Laura found and attended a Combinations training called Writing is Thinking (WIT 101)[1] for multilingual learners offered through the Hudson Valley Regional Bilingual Education Resource Network (HVRBERN[2]). At this training, Laura learned to develop her students' foundational academic literacy needs concurrently with grade-level content. But when she returned excited to share the strategies, her co-teachers were not interested or willing to try them with the whole class. Laura implemented Combinations where she could, here and there.

Hoping for camaraderie and also to eventually hold an administrative position where she could make a bigger difference, Laura joined a school building leadership certification program grounded in SI called Collaborative Leadership to Advance School Success (CLASS) offered through Hunter College at the City University of New York.[3] Laura joined a specialized cohort of CLASS that was offered in partnership with the HVRBERN and focused on developing leadership for multilingual learners. This cohort – taught by lead instructor Michelle Brochu with two senior staff members of the HVRBERN, Rachael Wasilewski-Alcantara and Beverly Guity – prioritized leadership to accelerate academic literacy for multilingual learners and included learning about Combinations. Thus, it was in this context of a multilingual learner-focused school building leadership certification program that Laura was supported deeply to implement and then to lead the spread of both SI and Combinations at Mountainview.

Learning to Move Students through Strategic Inquiry Plus Combinations

In CLASS, candidates learn SI by participating on a team with colleagues in the leadership cohort to improve performance for historically underserved and underperforming students in their schools during the first semester. During the second and third semesters, they lead the spread of improvement to colleagues and in their school systems (Panero & Talbert, 2013). Although Laura learned and enacted this work as part of a cohort team in an administrative program, for the purposes of this case study, we focus on her learning and work with her focal student and teachers at her school. Readers should note that the experience of the cohort team in the first semester of CLASS is meant to simulate the work of a school team. Therefore, readers should feel free to imagine that what Laura is learning and experiencing would typically be enacted by an entire school team as a collective. We focus on Laura as an individual in this case (rather than on the experiences of her cohort team) in order to get as granular as possible in our analysis.

The instructor team, led by Michelle Brochu, had determined up front that the strategic inquiry task of the first semester for Laura's entire cohort would be to improve writing performance on the NYSESLAT for specific struggling English learners. They made this decision based upon an understanding of trend data (that students typically scored the lowest on the writing section of the NYSESLAT across New York State) *and* based upon their understanding of leverage (that by introducing Combinations as a set of strategies to address writing challenges, students' performance across multiple NYSESLAT domains would likely improve).

After sharing the trend data and their rationale, Michelle and her co-instructors led their cohort teams to engage in the term's core inquiry task, which required Laura and her team to do the following, each of which is described (from Laura's perspective) below:

1. Identify target students and generate a specific, measurable long-term (semester-end) goal;
2. Identify smaller learning targets and sequence them in a plan to meet the long-term goal;
3. Engage in cycles of SI plus Combinations to move students to the long-term goal; and
4. Evaluate impact.

Identify Target Students and Generate a Specific, Measurable Long-Term Goal

First, Laura and her team were asked to identify one specific student each to study as a team. There were four teachers on this team, and thus there would be four target students. Each student must be someone they taught, who was designated as an EL, who had strong attendance (so they could test and learn from instructional interventions), who was struggling with writing and with academics generally and who represented larger challenges in the school so that what was learned could benefit more students.

Laura selected Salvador, a student in her fourth-grade class who had come to Mountainview from Mexico in Kindergarten but who was still scoring as *emerging* (a beginner score) on the NYSESLAT. Salvador was a delightful boy. He came to school every day eager to learn and participated enthusiastically. He had many friends, and his social language in English was strong. But in reading and writing in English, he was far below grade level. The problem was certainly made worse by the pandemic, as school for the prior two years had been largely remote and Salvador did not have access to English language support at home. But this wasn't the whole story. Even before the pandemic, Laura knew, beginner ELs at Mountainview were not making needed progress.

Laura and her colleagues were asked to establish a measurable and specific long-term (semester-end) goal for their target students as a driver of their inquiry work for the term. This process required active facilitation by the instructors, who modeled a process for using a sample NYSESLAT prompt to generate a baseline writing sample for target students; scoring the sample with the NYSESLAT writing rubric, sticking closely to the student work as evidence; zooming in to select *ONE* high-leverage dimension on this rubric as a priority area of focus for the inquiry work all term; and crafting a long-term measurable movement goal within this one high-leverage dimension as their long-term (semester-end) goal. You can find sample NYSESLAT materials, including writing rubrics, at https://www.nysedregents.org/nyseslat/2019/nyseslat19-turnkey-training-binderw.pdf.

To secure Salvador's baseline, Laura provided a third–fourth grade sample NYSESLAT prompt that required Salvador to read a few paragraphs about travel in the 1800s and then write his own paragraph comparing travel in the 1800s with travel today.

Salvador's response can be seen in Figure 8.1.

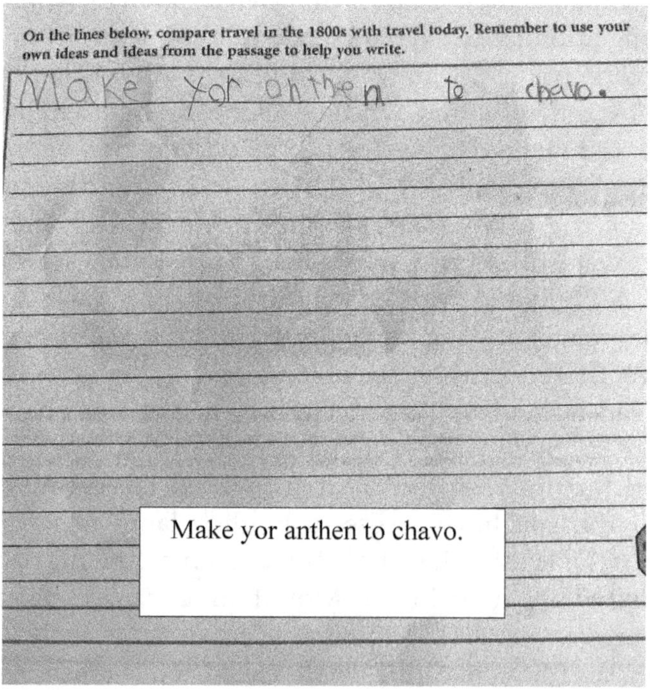

> On the lines below, compare travel in the 1800s with travel today. Remember to use your own ideas and ideas from the passage to help you write.
>
> Make yor anthen to chavo.

FIGURE 8.1 Salvador's baseline response to NYSESLAT prompt about comparing travel in the 1800s to today.

Image courtesy of Salvador.

To score their baseline writing samples, the team studied and came to deeply understand the language requirements in the writing section of the NYSESLAT rubric. They scored Salvador's writing as a zero (*entering*), determining that it fit the rubric's description of *entering* because it included mostly Tier 1 words, lacked development of a thought or idea, lacked description of clear facts and contained words or an overall meaning that was unclear.

After providing scores for each of the four target students (all of whom were either entering or emerging), the team set about to select their *ONE* high-leverage dimension *AND* to generate a challenging but achievable long-term goal, the amount of progress the team would aim for in that dimension by the end of the term.

Laura and her team selected a dimension of the NYSESLAT writing rubric, *Complexity of Language*, which required students to write simple and then expanded and/or complex sentences. It seemed to be the area that was most needed by their students and that could potentially lead to broader improvements across the rubric.

Finally, the team created a measurable and challenging but achievable long-term (semester-end) goal in *Complexity of Language*. Salvador, Laura and her team decided, would move two points on the rubric, from *entering* to *transitioning*. Laura's work for the term – to move Salvador from entering to transitioning on the NYSESLAT writing rubric, was now clear. Each team member had a similar goal – to move their target students from one to two levels in *Complexity of Language*.

Identify Smaller Learning Targets and Sequence Them in a Plan to Meet the Long-Term Goal

Although Laura and her team had identified *writing simple and then expanded or complex sentences* as their goal, they did not feel confident that they would be able to meet it. After all, seeing that their students scored at the beginning level was nothing new for these teachers. They'd been trying their best for many years to address this problem. So, they wondered what was going to be different this time.

Typically, what Laura and her colleagues would do, after seeing a beginning score, was to use the information on the existing rubric to guide their decisions about what to teach next. If they saw only Tier 1 words in the students' writing, for example, they would teach more Tier 2 vocabulary, since this was called for on the rubric. If they saw a lack of description or development of ideas, as called for on the rubric, they would work on students' writing development.

As the next step in the SI process, however, Michelle, and her co-instructors, pointed the teams in a different direction. Instead of asking them to move directly to interventions, they asked the teams to drill down further in their assessments. To do so, Michelle provided a tool called a "Sentence Tracker" which had been generated in earlier SI work and provided a way for teachers to identify more precise sentence-level strengths and needs. It is designed so that each item on the tracker maps to Combinations strategies to address it (item 1 corresponds to *boundaries* strategies; item 2 to *sentence types*; item 3 to *BBS* and so on). Note that the skills in items 7 and 8 are addressed across Combinations. Michelle told the teachers that each item corresponded to a set of strategies, and that she would be introducing those strategies as needed.

Laura and her team analyzed their target students' NYSESLAT baseline writing samples with the sentence tracker. The results (all Ns) are displayed in Figure 8.2.

As a result of this initial scoring, however, the team was still at a bit of a loss. They liked the idea of getting more granular evidence than the initial rubric provided to inform their next steps. But their tracker was filled with Ns, so they still didn't have the information they needed to know where to begin. Their first inclination was to start with sentence boundaries, since it was first on the tracker. But Michelle coached them through questioning to shift from taking action with incomplete information to generating even more granular assessments. "What skills do your kids need first to even get to number one on the sentence tracker?" Michelle asked, showing them an example of a "pre-sentence tracker" that had been created by an inquiry team at a school she had worked with.

"Oh!" the team members said. Now unstuck, they created a pre-sentence tracker that included skills such as sound-letter

Sentence Tracker – Indicates where to begin with sentences
1. Answer each of the following questions with a Yes (Y) or No (N) in the boxes below.
2. Count the number of N's and record (in the bottom row and right-hand column).
3. What patterns do you see? Who struggles most? What skills do students struggle with most?
4. Where will you begin and with whom (how might you adjust your target population)?

		Student 1	Student 2	Student 3	Student 4	Student 5	Student 6	Total N's per skill
Sentence Skills	1. Is there evidence of mastery of sentence boundaries (all complete sentences, no fragments or run-ons)?	N	N	N	N			
	2. Is there evidence of the ability to vary sentence types (for ex., use of question or exclamation)?	N	N	N	N			
	3. Is there evidence of mastery of use of the coordinating conjunctions but, because and so?	N	N	N	N			
	4. Is there evidence of mastery of the appositive (use of at least one appositive?)	N	N	N	N			
	5. Is there evidence of mastery of varied sentence starters (any sentences that begin with a subordinating conjunction, such as since, if, after, or although)?	N	N	N	N			
	6. Are sentences elaborated with rich detail answering questions such as who, when, how and why - beyond the bare minimum required for a simple sentence?	N	N	N	N			
	7. Is there varied, precise (content-specific, academic) vocabulary?	N	N	N	N			
	8. Is there evidence of mastery of mechanics (capitalization, punctuation, subject verb agreement, tense agreement, etc)?	N	N	N	N			
	Total N's per student:	8	8	8	8			

FIGURE 8.2 Sentence tracker analyzing student baseline writing sample.

correspondence, spelling, proper spacing between letters and writing a simple sentence that has a subject and a predicate. There were younger target students that were missing more of these skills than Salvador was; but in her work, Laura found that there was direct instruction that Salvador needed, for example, to master sound-letter correspondence for some of letters. Laura worked on sound-letter correspondence and the basics of a simple sentence with Salvador (whom she had come to call by his nickname, Sal) for three weeks, during which time she moved him from ten Ns to three Ns on this pre-sentence tracker. Then, Laura felt, she and Sal were ready to tackle the sentence tracker.

Drawing on her knowledge from Combinations training and the new overview provided by Michelle, Laura had a sense of how best to sequence Combinations instruction. Michelle provided an additional tool – the planning staircase (see Figure 8.3) – to

148 ◆ What It Looks Like on the Ground

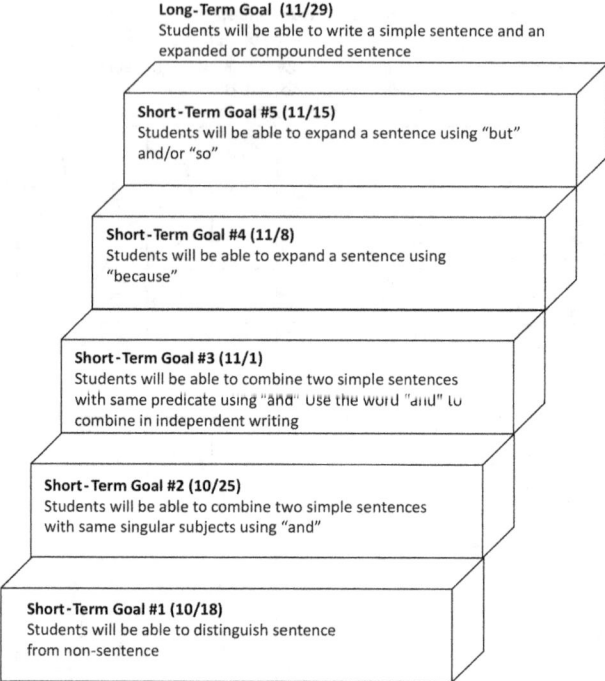

FIGURE 8.3 The planning staircase depicting Laura's plan for Sal.

Planning staircase courtesy of Michelle Brochu.

support the team's planning of interim goals with dates as a roadmap. Each team member had the same long-term goal and an individualized staircase for their target student. Laura's staircase (plan for Sal) can be seen in Figure 8.3.

Laura summarized the backward-design thinking process that she and her team had gone through in order to create Sal's staircase as follows:

> We thought about what we wanted students to accomplish (write a simple sentence and an expanded or complex sentence), and then we thought about what skills they would need prior to being able to accomplish this goal independently. We thought that combining would be easier than expanding sentences using *because, but & so* because teachers frequently ask students to elaborate with more information by using the question word "why" after they wrote sentences.

By breaking up each of these conjunctions we were able to directly target specific language functions and structures in the students' spoken and written discourse. We also knew that in order for students to be able to accomplish any sentence level task, they needed to be able to articulate and explain what a sentence was and what it was not, which would be accomplished through sorting.

Engage in Cycles of Strategic Inquiry Plus Combinations to Move Students to the Long-Term Goal

With their roadmaps (staircases) in hand, Laura and her team tackled their short-term goals one by one, in each case by implementing targeted Combinations activities that served simultaneously as teaching tools and as formative assessments; the work produced by the students informed their next teaching and inquiry steps. When students did not provide evidence of meeting the specific short-term goal, the interventions and, if needed, the timelines (staircases) were adjusted in response.

For example, Laura's first attempt to support Sal in identifying sentences versus non-sentences within academic content was not successful, and she had to change course. Laura had followed what she learned at Combinations training. First, she provided strips that contained simple sentences and non-sentences using familiar vocabulary – sentence strips like "Juan is a good friend". She asked Sal to sort the strips into piles: Sentence or Not a Sentence. Sal was able to do this. Then she provided a similar activity using content and language from *The Wind in the Willows*.

This time, Sal had trouble. He looked at the strips and sort of froze, "a little like a deer in headlights", Laura said. He started to get up and move to another part of the room. When Laura sat with Sal to work on the activity together, he seemed to be guessing and was not able to apply what he knew when the activity used familiar language. Sal's trouble was probably a result of the more sophisticated academic vocabulary, Laura reasoned. For the first sentence strip ("Rat is a loyal friend"), she had intentionally selected the word "loyal" instead of "good". For the second strip ("Rat and Mole arrive at Toad's mansion"), she had chosen "mansion" instead of "house". Both "loyal" and "mansion" were important words for understanding the subtleties of meaning in the novel they were studying. In the past, if her students struggled, she would stick to simpler language. But she knew that Combinations was designed to allow access to grade-level content despite one's level of English language proficiency. She had directly taught the meaning of "loyal" and "mansion" when reading and discussing *The Wind in the Willows*, but clearly Sal was still confused. What should she do next?

When Laura shared her struggle with the entire cohort at the next session, a class member suggested that she try the same activity first in Sal's home language. "If he sees the words in Spanish first, that might just free up his mental energy to focus on the sentence structure, and then to transfer what he knows about the vocabulary and the structure into English", she explained. Laura decided to give this a shot. The following week she provided the same activity first in Spanish and then shortly afterward in English (see Figure 8.4), adjusting her staircase accordingly. And it worked.

"This was a big Aha! Moment for Sal, and for me!" Laura explained.

> Having it in his home language just really seemed to unlock things for Sal. He said 'Oh! This is how this works!' Maybe it was because he wasn't thrown off by the words he didn't know in English. I'm not sure. But he was able to see in his native language how the way we organize words can create or not create a sentence. He saw that if there isn't a subject and predicate, the sentence doesn't make sense, so it's a fragment. Then he could transfer this knowledge of word order and structure into English.

This experience solidified for Laura what she had learned about using as in students' home language as a bridge in Combinations. "This is what the research says", Laura said. "But I had never really seen it with my own eyes, the way having the activity presented in home language could unlock so much for Sal".

As Laura began to have success, she shared what she was seeing with her co-teacher, Christine, and asked if she wanted

A Case Study (The Nitty Gritty of the What, How and to What Effect) ◆ 151

Sentence strips in English
- Rat is a loyal friend
- Rat and Mole arrive at Toad's mansion
- rich and nice
- Mole and Rat
- the cart is broken

Sentence strips in Spanish:
- Rata es un amigo leal
- Rata y Topo llegaron a la mansión de Sapo
- Rico y agradable
- Topo y Rata
- La carreta está rota

FIGURE 8.4 Example of sentence strips in both the home language of Spanish and in English.

to work together to implement some of the strategies with the whole class. "It sounds great", Christine said. But I just don't have time because there's all these other things I have to do with the new curriculum!" So Laura went along doing them on the side, just with Sal.

When Sal was ready, Laura moved to short-term goal number 2: Combining two simple sentences with a similar simple subject and the word "and", as in Sal's example in Figure 8.5.

And then to short-term goal number 3: Combining two simple sentences with the same predicate using "and" AND using "and" independently, as in the example in Figure 8.6.

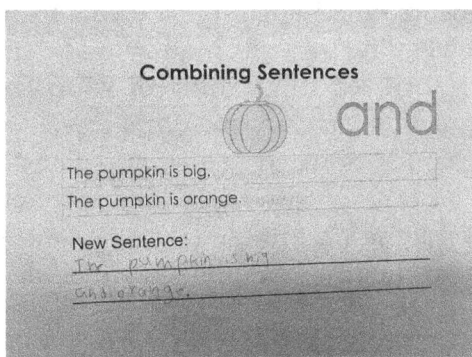

FIGURE 8.5 Sal's response when asked to combine two simple sentences with a similar simple subject and the word "and".

Image courtesy of Salvador.

152 ◆ What It Looks Like on the Ground

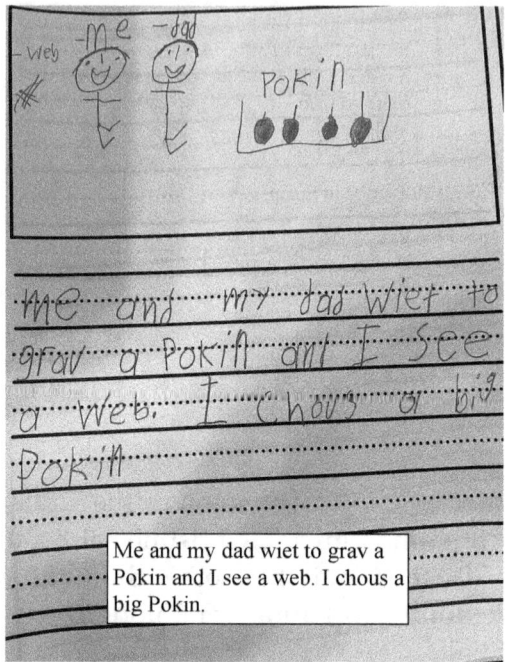

Me and my dad wiet to grav a Pokin and I see a web. I chous a big Pokin.

FIGURE 8.6 Example of Sal's work for short-term goal number 3: Combining two simple sentences with the same predicate using "and" AND using "and" independently.

Image courtesy of Salvador.

Throughout the process, Laura and her team were coached by the instructors to use the driving end goal in determining instructional priorities. In NYSESLAT scoring, students are not scored lower for invented spelling or errors in mechanics that do not impede meaning. In their inquiry work, therefore, Laura and her team prioritized the writing of varied sentence forms over other linguistic elements, including mechanics. They did not ignore mechanics, however. This particular piece of writing (in Figure 8.6), for example, prompted Laura to reinforce the use of a capital letter at the start of each sentence and a period at the end. But when an interim goal aligned to the driving end goal was met, the instruction moved along the staircase accordingly. In this case, Sal had indeed mastered the second part of interim goal number 3: independent application of the word "and" to produce a compound sentence!

Laura moved on in a similar fashion to goal 4, again first in familiar language and then in the content Sal was studying. One example of a "because" task Laura created about *The Wind in the Willows* was: "Toad is irresponsible because…" and "Mole is a good friend because…". When Sal demonstrated proficiency, Laura moved on to *but*. Like with many students, Salvador had a pretty easy time with *because* and *but*, but needed more explicit reinforcement and instruction to grasp the more complex cause-effect relationship indicated by *so*.

As this was happening (in mid-November), something started to change with Laura's co-teacher, Christine. One day Christine said to Laura:

> What you're doing with Sal, it's really showing up in other parts of the day, like in Math. He used *because* when he explained his math answer yesterday. What you're doing is really working! I think we need to do it with the whole class.

Laura had noticed that there was a WIT training coming up the first week in December, and not missing a beat, she asked Christine if she wanted to attend with her. "I need a refresher", Laura explained, "and we could learn together". Christine agreed, and the principal approved their attendance. Attending WIT together marked a big transition in their co-teaching relationship. After the training, Laura and Christine co-planned and co-taught, often with Laura at the helm. Following Laura's lead, Christine selected two more target students – Angel and Krismel – to begin focusing upon intensively the next semester and whose progress she would closely track.

Evaluate Impact

Laura and her team knew their target students were making progress. They saw it every day! But they were still nervous when they gave their post-assessments at the end of the term. Would their students meet the long-term goal? In December, Laura asked Sal to write in response to the same prompt she had given him in September. In December, what Sal wrote can be seen in Figure 8.7.

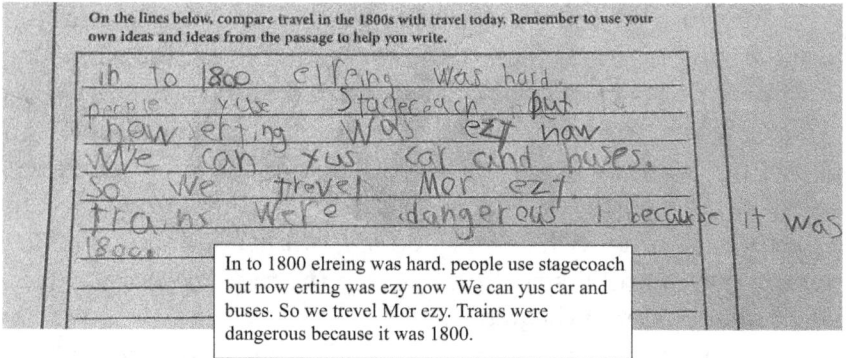

FIGURE 8.7 Sal's post-assessment response to NYSESLAT prompt about comparing travel in the 1800s to today.

Image courtesy of Salvador.

On a first read, Laura and her team were thrilled to see that Sal had met their top-of-the-staircase goal by writing at least one expanding or complex sentence and thereby earning a score of *transitioning* in *Complexity of Language*. When they looked more closely, however, they realized that Sal had actually surpassed this goal – that his response now met the requirements of the *expanding* level in *Complexity of Language* because it included both an expanded *and* a complex sentence. Sal's first sentence was complex: "In the 1800s, everything was hard". Two of his sentences were expanded because they answered the question *why*, as in "Trains were dangerous because it was the 1800s".

What Laura and her team definitely did not expect was that by focusing small – on one dimension and a small set of strategies – Sal and other target students would improve not only on the targeted dimension but on the writing rubric overall. Sal moved up two levels in each dimension, now scoring as *transitioning* on the writing rubric overall. All four target students met or surpassed their long-term goal.

Laura and Christine were similarly "blown away" by the range of effects they were seeing in the classroom. "The work we did wasn't just about writing", Laura explained.

It's about all the language domains! Because of the repeated exposures he got to the sentence structures and the vocabulary,

Sal started reading aloud in class! He was reading better, and he was understanding more in the reading and in spoken language in class. Plus, he was using the structures in his own language. Like Christine said, he was using *because* in Math!

Christine had already come on board. But when she saw how the strategies transferred to varied subjects and to Sal's post-assessment, along with how his confidence as a student had improved, she was truly hooked.

When Laura and Christine presented Sal's progress at his parent-teacher conference in January, showing his before and after writing samples, Sal's parents were thrilled. "Just keep doing what you're doing!" they said. And when Laura asked Sal if he was happy about his progress, about what he was able to write now, he nodded and beamed. "What's changed from here to here", Laura asked Sal, placing his pre- and post-assessment writing in front of him and pressing Sal to show her his level of understanding about his own growth and progress. "I don't like this one", Sal said, picking up his September writing. "Let's throw it away". "No, we're not going to throw it out!" Laura said. "It shows us how much you have learned, and I'm so proud of you! What do you think is different?" "The first time I started writing, I was scared and I only write a little bit", Sal said. "I write more now. I write more sentences".

At the end of the year, Sal scored at the transitioning level on the NYSESLAT assessment as a whole, moving up to transitioning in one year after having been stuck at emerging for three. "Salvador was on track to becoming a long-term EL", Laura said. "But not anymore!"

Spreading the Work

In January, the SST selected Angel and Krismel as two of the students to focus upon in the Spring. Laura, as a member of the SST, was present for the team's selection of students. And she was distressed, as usual, when she heard SST members talk about these students as if they were incapable of making progress. "Look at the data", the reading teacher had said. "I really think they need to be in special ed".

Laura and Christine approached the SST with a plan. They briefly explained the training they had attended together and its impact along with how it could be implemented in the context of the school's tiered intervention system. They provided a rationale for a focus on writing (how writing could leverage improvement across the language modalities), which had never been done before; typically, the SST focused on reading. And they proposed to lead the SST through SI plus Combinations with Christine implementing Tier 1 intervention with the entire class; Laura implementing Tier 2 interventions with select students in and out of class, and with both implementing Tier 3 (additional outside class) interventions as needed. Though the SST was skeptical, Laura's and Christine's passion – and the data they showed about Sal – convinced them to give it a try. Laura and Christine even convinced the SST to meet for eight sessions rather than the usual six, the minimum they felt was required to get enough headway with Combinations that results would transfer to a long-term goal.

In eight bi-weekly sessions over three months (from February to May), Laura led the SST through the SI plus Combinations process that she had experienced with equally successful results. In the first few sessions, Laura led the team first to explore the NYSESLAT. This took longer than expected, since – as Laura learned – nobody understood the language requirements of this assessment. Next, she led them to score the baseline writing samples with the NYSESLAT writing rubric and the sentence tracker. Then she introduced Combinations and led the team to generate a staircase plan to guide their work, as seen in Figure 8.8.

Over the next set of sessions, Laura led the team through cycles of implementation and analysis, during which time all team members, including Laura and Christine, became increasingly skilled in adapting Combinations and instruction in response to Combinations-based formative assessment. Although both Laura and Christine drew upon their prior experiences and training and served in leadership roles, they were also learners, as nobody knew quite where the evidence would lead.

"The real nail biting moment was the last session", Laura explained. "We had seen the students making incremental progress,

A Case Study (The Nitty Gritty of the What, How and to What Effect) ◆ 157

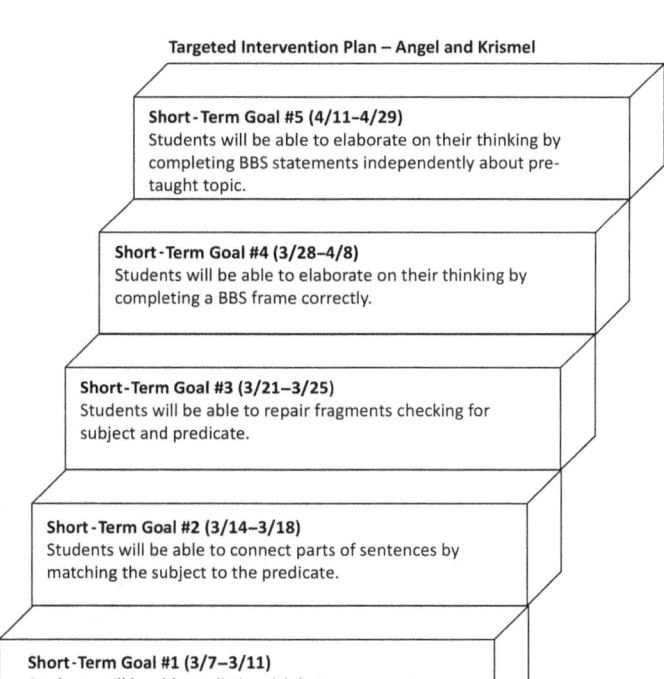

FIGURE 8.8 The planning staircase depicts SST's plan for Angel and Krismel.

Planning staircase courtesy of Michelle Brochu.

but we hadn't taken a step back to look at the whole picture. When we saw the results of Angel's and Krismel's post assessments, the teachers were really blown away".

Like Sal, after approximately three months of work, Angel and Krismel moved up two levels in *Complexity of Language* (from entering to expanding) and one level (to transitioning) on the writing rubric overall. Also, like for Sal, these improvements showed up in the year-end NYSESLAT. The SST was stunned. Yes, they had seen the students making progress, but "to see the big payoff on the post assessment was a whole other thing". After the final NYSESLAT scores were in, Christine presented to the SST and she said in pointing to the data display, "You can see that their Coherence of Response has improved as well". "I sound so smart now", Christine said to Laura later. "This work makes me feel and sound so smart". "You were always smart",

Laura replied. "It's just that now you are using the language of the rubric to explain your thinking". Most importantly, nobody still thought that the students should be evaluated for special education. The standing SST team members asked Laura and Christine to present their work to the principal.

The following year, when Angel and Krismel had been assigned to different teachers, but were still a focus of the SST, the SST asked Christine and Laura to attend the first SST meeting to share their approach and progress. "We can't have everything that you did just get lost", one of the counselor members of the SST said.

When Laura and Christine presented in September of the following year, Angel's and Krismel's new co-teachers (a general education and an EL teacher) were impressed. When Laura and Christine offered to teach them about Combinations and/or to meet with them regularly to do some inquiry, the general education teacher said: "it sounds really great, but I just don't think I have time". The EL teacher however sought out Laura separately and made time to meet with her. And something similar happened to what had happened with Laura and Christine: about one month into the work, the co-teacher said: "Something that you're doing is really working. Can I learn more about it?"

Laura and Christine are working to gradually expand the work in this fashion, through word of mouth and teachers' seeing the results. For Angel's and Krismel's before and after writing samples, see Figures 8.9–8.14:

Figures 8.9–8.14: Angel's and Krismel's Writing over Time

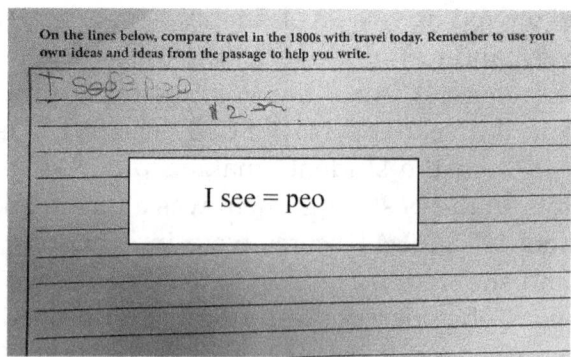

FIGURE 8.9 Angel's first baseline (September 2021).

Image courtesy of Angel.

A Case Study (The Nitty Gritty of the What, How and to What Effect) ◆ 159

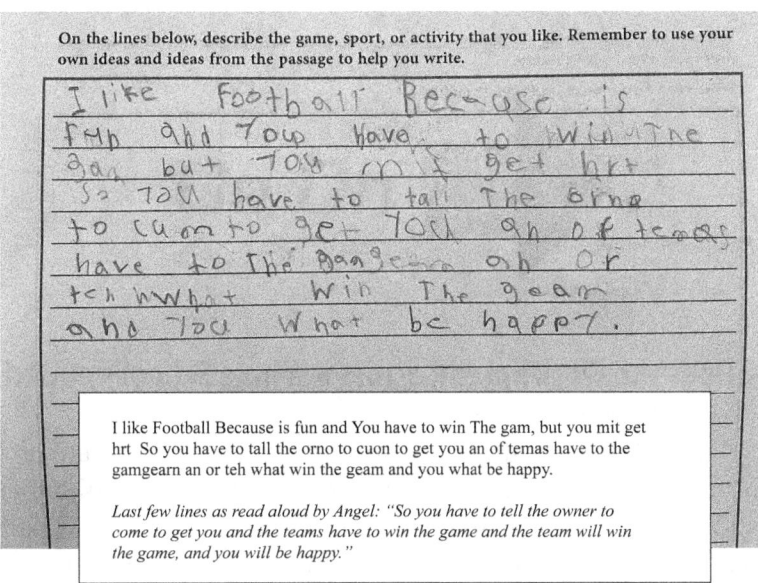

I like to play football because you run I like

FIGURE 8.10 Angel's new baseline (February 2022 – Note that Angel and Krismel benefitted from the whole-class Combinations work Laura and Christine began in December 2021).

Image courtesy of Angel.

I like Football Because is fun and You have to win The gam, but you mit get hrt So you have to tall the orno to cuon to get you an of temas have to the gamgearn an or teh what win the geam and you what be happy.

Last few lines as read aloud by Angel: "So you have to tell the owner to come to get you and the teams have to win the game and the team will win the game, and you will be happy."

FIGURE 8.11 Angel's post-assessment (April 2022).

Image courtesy of Angel.

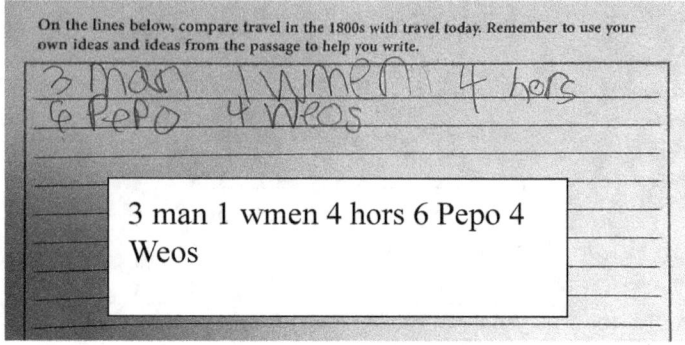

FIGURE 8.12 Krismel's first Baseline (September 2021).

Image courtesy of Krismel.

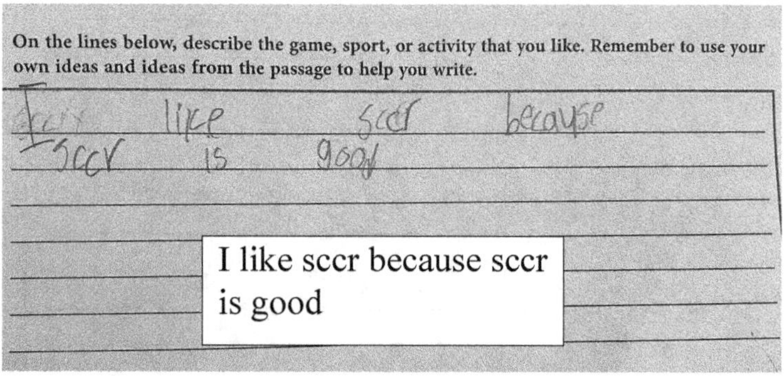

FIGURE 8.13 Krismel's second baseline (February 2022).

Image courtesy of Krismel.

How Does the Work Spread across a Whole School or District?

We selected this case study to highlight what it looks like on the ground and up close when a teacher is learning to implement SI plus Combinations with students; and to show how a teacher, regardless of their level of positional authority, can be a lever for change by demonstrating results and leading the spread gradually. We want to show that authentic buy-in comes gradually, as teachers demonstrate results, and entails slow and incremental professional learning initially. This process is worth the time it takes because it counters the typical impediments to change

A Case Study (The Nitty Gritty of the What, How and to What Effect) ◆ 161

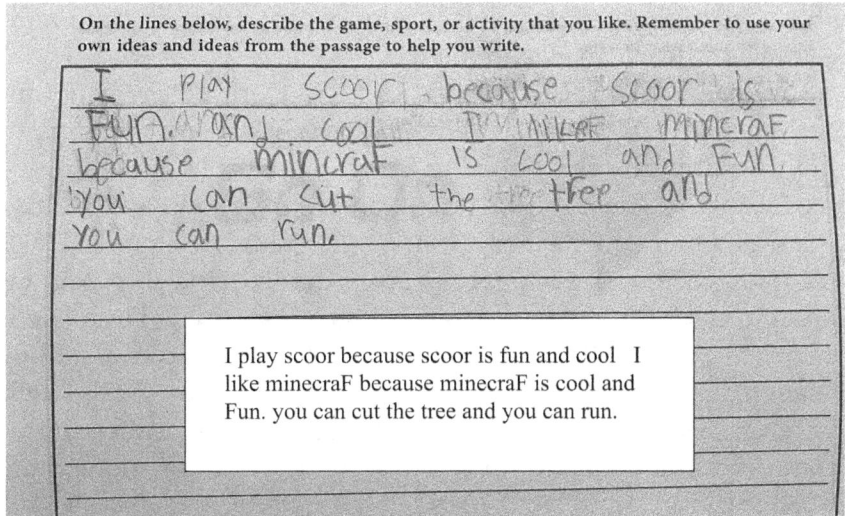

FIGURE 8.14 Krismel's post-assessment (April 2022).

Image courtesy of Krismel.

(including belief systems about whose job it is to address the needs of multilingual learners) through a real grounded process that is built to last.

There is no question, however, that to accelerate the spread of this work and to enable it to take hold across an entire school or district – which is of course ideal – requires understanding, commitment and support from formal leaders. What's most important for a building-level leader is the understanding that learning to implement this work takes time. Teachers must be provided with the opportunity to learn Combinations through professional development over time (see Endnote 1 in Chapter 1 for options) and with time to meet collaboratively for an inquiry process. The principal should learn alongside teachers and become familiar with the strategies, as should others who supervise instruction, so they understand what to hold teachers accountable for. Up front knowledge is not necessary, as long as there is an understanding that learning will take time and a commitment to engaging in it over time. Similarly, district leaders do not need to be deeply knowledgeable about Combinations or SI up front;

what's necessary is the allocation and protection of time and resources to learn and to do the work.

Deirdre DeAngelis, principal of New Dorp High School in Staten Island, NY, was an incredible building leader who strategically and skillfully committed to Combinations plus SI as a strategy for instructional improvement and saw striking and steady progress, moving her school from a 54% graduation rate in 2005 to 89% in 2022, when she retired from the Principalship. For an in-depth case study of the spread of this work at New Dorp High School, see pages 83–105 in *Strategic inquiry: Starting Small for Big Results In Education* (Panero & Talbert, 2013). This New Dorp High School case study makes clear how school building leadership is key in creating the conditions within which Combinations plus SI can thrive.

Aimee Horowitz, District Superintendent of the New York City Department of Education (NYCDOE) Renewal High Schools, committed to a similar process for forging improvement in NYC DOE's 35 renewal (identified by New York State as struggling) high schools between 2014 and 2016 (Wohlstetter et al., 2018). Like Principal DeAngelis, Superintendent Horowitz created a learning culture. First, she provided professional development to teachers in Combinations. Then, she layered in a train-the-facilitator structure for additional support. In the first year, select teacher facilitators from each school attended monthly full-day training sessions to learn SI tools deeply and to be supported to lead SI teams at their schools. In the second year, these facilitators coached newly selected teachers to lead SI teams as they took on and received support to address new challenges. The evaluation found that very positive results were achieved rapidly and inexpensively. Through a streamlined district intervention, researchers found, students in participating schools were brought on track to graduation two times more than similar students in similar non-SI schools and were almost two and a half more times likely to graduate, with results most noticeable for special education students and multilingual learners (Wohlstetter et al., 2018).

Most radical and essential in these and other cases of successful school and district-wide implementation was the leaders' understanding of the power of small strategies to leverage a large difference, and of the space they then created and protected for teachers and coaches/facilitators to learn new strategies deeply. For the first full year of implementation of a comprehensive writing program at New Dorp, DeAngelis supported – even required – her teachers to focus on sentences. She did this despite strong pockets of resistance, given pending essay-based state exams that students were required to pass to graduate. It takes courage rooted in high expectations (the conviction that student performance is a mirror of teacher practice, and thus that when teacher practice improves, so too will student performance) as well as an understanding of how Combinations leverages so much to push back on the pressures on teachers and schools to go big from the start. Superintendent Horowitz also prioritized sentence learning for the first full year, which was incredible – we, the authors, believe – given the spotlight on this high-stakes initiative and the pressure to produce results quickly, as typically measured by graduation rates. Early on, Horowitz demonstrated her commitment to the approach and its theory of change when she said – to an assembled group of approximately 90 teachers at the first Combinations workshop – "We are going to start small to make a big difference!" This commitment paid off.

Conclusion

Research tells us a lot about *what* conditions must be in place in order for change efforts in education to take hold, but much less about *how* to bring these conditions into being. What we hope to make clear in this chapter is how SI plus Combinations can bring coherence among the many needed elements within an ecosystem in support of educational change. We show how SI plus Combinations operates to develop needed skills and habits of mind at every level of the system and to organize and bring coherence in support of multilingual learners' success. We hope to show as well how doing so paves the way for the spread and development of instructional practices and a school culture that supports all students.

Combinations strategies are powerful on their own. SI is as well. What we hope this case study makes clear, however, is that when joined, Combinations becomes far more than a recipe for improving student writing. When implemented in the context of SI, teachers learn a scaffolded investigative process that leads students to learn skills that are broadly applicable and the teachers themselves learn how to learn. What's important for Sal, for example, is not that he's learned to write a compound sentence about a pumpkin. What's important is that he has learned a set of function words (discourse markers) and how they operate that he can apply independently and broadly to a wide variety of circumstances and situations. He can use *because* to explain mathematical thinking. He can deploy *so* in writing to express cause and effect. He can deduce meaning and complexity when these discourse markers are present in academic text. Most importantly, perhaps, he has metalinguistic awareness about his own language-use; he can talk and think about his own literacy practice.

Similarly, what's important for Laura and her colleagues is not that they have learned to implement a menu of Combinations strategies. What's more important are the fundamental shifts in what they pay attention to, their mindsets and how they teach. In the past, Laura paid a lot of attention to the curriculum and to the end tasks that the curriculum required. If the curriculum required that students write a paragraph about *The Wind in the Willows* (Grahame, 1989), she would focus on teaching students to write a paragraph. Now Laura focuses on what knowledge effectively completing a task requires and on where her students are in a developmental continuum of being able to complete that task. She continuously assesses in order to target the just-right teaching point (Vygotsky & Cole, 1978) to allow incremental success and gradual independence along this continuum. In a word, what SI plus Combinations has allowed for Laura and her colleagues is an understanding of how to put into practice what they've read about in the research and learned about in their educational teaching programs regarding pedagogy for multilingual learners and all students: responsive teaching. It enables teachers to embody the elements of high-quality teaching for ELs (see Chapter 7).

For those like Christine who questioned the ability of multilingual learners to thrive academically and her own ability to help them do so, SI plus Combinations can help educators change course, seeding self-efficacy, confidence and a sense of urgency for supporting multilingual learners' success that is infectious and can spread across a school and district.

Notes

1 For more information about WIT, see www.strategicinquiry.com
2 For more information about the HVRBERN, see https://www.hudson valleyrbern.org/
3 See https://education.hunter.cuny.edu/admissions/graduate-programs/leadership-programs/class-program/

References

Grahame, K. (1989). *The wind in the willows*. Aladdin Paperbacks.

Panero, N. S., & Talbert, J. E. (2013). *Strategic inquiry: Starting small for big results in education*. Harvard Education Press.

Vygotsky, L. S., & Cole, M. (1978). *Mind in society: Development of higher psychological processes*. Harvard University Press.

Wohlstetter, P., Kim, E., Flack, C. B., & Mat, A. (2018). Strategic inquiry and New York City's renewal high schools. *Teachers College Columbia University, November*. https://www.tc.columbia.edu/media/news/images/2018/december/Wohlstetter_Strategic-Inquiry-Final-Report-1.0-1.pdf

9
Call to Action

The urgency to support culturally and linguistically diverse students, especially students identified as English Learners, in academic success is greater than ever before. Educators now also have more tools and knowledge to do so: high-quality instructional materials that are aligned to rigorous learning standards and shown to make a difference in student achievement (Koedel & Polikoff, 2017); a variety of high-quality training and resources for all teachers – not just language specialists – to develop the skills and practices they need in the classroom (Darling-Hammond et al., 2017) and increased shared accountability at the classroom, school, district, state and federal levels through the Every Student Succeeds Act.

Yet, even with these developments, the ability to change and improve at scale for multilingual learner success remains elusive in many local contexts. Many teachers learn about research-based best practices to support multilingual learners, but struggle to prioritize all that is asked of them and to implement these practices in ways that make the needed difference for students. In addition, many schools and districts do not have strong systems to get to the bottom of what multilingual learners – particularly students identified as English Learners – need, making it very challenging to sustain instructional wins beyond one teacher or classroom.

In this book, we have shown that when teachers have a laser focus on language and literacy in targeted ways – by focusing on the small but mighty sentence through Combinations – they are able to support learning for multilingual learners in many ways at once (content, literacy and thinking), and thus Combinations is a powerful accelerant for student learning through improved teacher practice. We have also shown that when Combinations is coupled with Strategic Inquiry (SI), a proven method for teacher teaming which includes targeting the precise areas in which changes in teacher practice are required to ensure student success and supporting teachers to see the need for and to make the needed changes, we see multiplier effects that drive improvement. That is, Combinations and SI together provide a powerful way forward because they bring content learning, academic literacy and adult development together in an effective and efficient manner. As we hope we have demonstrated in our case study of Mountainview in Chapter 8, Combinations and SI can work together to bring about the changes in thinking, practice and structure that constitute the culture changes we need to support multilingual learners' success in schools.

If you are a teacher or leader hoping to get started with the methods that we promote, here's what we suggest.

If you are a teacher, even without access to a collaborative team and even without administrative support, you can implement Combinations in your classroom. We recommend that you start small, with one or two strategies that best serve your students' needs and your content. As we have argued, implementing Combinations, even in situations that are less than ideal, will lead to rapid gains in students' writing, oral language, reading comprehension and engagement. It will also improve your teaching by providing a concrete way to integrate content and literacy instruction to pinpoint the needed next steps and to track progress.

The information we provide is more than enough to get you started and to make great progress with and beyond multilingual learners. Find at least one colleague to work with as a thought partner, if you can. It's extremely helpful to have a second set of eyes when you are designing tasks and to talk to as you explore how best to adapt the strategies to your classroom. If you find yourself wanting additional support, you might want to attend a Combinations-based professional development workshop.[1]

If you are a member of a collaborative team, we recommend that you consider introducing Combinations as a focus of the team's work, as there is strong evidence that Combinations and inquiry can amplify each other's impact. There is evidence, in other words, that a structured inquiry process helps Combinations to take hold and that Combinations can make inquiry more effective. For those looking to get started implementing this pairing, you may find the "Where do I begin" tool and the "Sentence Tracker" (Appendices A and B) helpful, as well as the vignette in Chapter 1 and the case study in Chapter 8, which illustrate how these tools can be used in practice. We also recommend the book *Strategic Inquiry: Starting Small for Big Results in Education* (Panero & Talbert, 2013) or to join a virtual SI plus Combinations team.[2]

If you are a school or district administrator, you are in a position to create the structures that will most powerfully support this work. In this case, we suggest the integration of Combinations with SI in the design of your work up front. Most importantly, we suggest a design that allows for sufficient and ongoing learning for all those involved and that there is a concrete plan for facilitator development, which is an essential and often under-appreciated and under-invested requirement for success (Panero, 2021). If at any point along this journey you think a conversation with us would be helpful, please reach out.

While learning to implement Combinations with SI is not easy, we hope you will come to see, as we have time and again, that investing in this change strategy is well worth the effort because it pays off in multiplier effects for students, teachers and school systems. We hope you will come to see as we have its transformative power in support of multilingual learners' success.

Notes

1 See https://strategicinquiry.com/workshops/
2 For more information or to sign up to join a virtual SI plus Combinations team, see https://strategicinquiry.com

References

Darling-Hammond, L., Hyler, M. E., & Gardner, M. (2017). Effective teacher professional development. *Learning Policy Institute.* https://learningpolicyinstitute.org/product/effective-teacher-professional-development-report

Koedel, C., & Polikoff, M. (2017). Big bang for just a few bucks: The impact of math textbooks in California. *Evidence Speaks Reports*, *2*(5), 1–7.

Panero, N. S. (2021). Shifting team culture: An analysis of effective facilitator moves in inquiry-based reform. *Leadership and Policy in Schools*, 1–13. https://doi.org/10.1080/15700763.2021.1977334

Panero, N. S., & Talbert, J. E. (2013). *Strategic inquiry: Starting small for big results in education*. Harvard Education Press.

Appendix A

Tracker to Assess Student Paragraph and Sentence Skills

Where Should We Begin: Paragraph or Sentence?

Assess each students' paragraph using the chart below.
1. Place a **Y** or **N** in each box.
2. Count the number of "N"s for Categories A and B.
3. Decide where to begin:
- If you have more "N"s in Category A - begin inquiry work with paragraph skills.
- If you have more "N"s in Category B - begin inquiry work with sentence skills.

		Student 1	Student 2	Student 3	Student 4	Student 5	Student 6	Student 7	Student 8	Student 9	Student 10
A. Paragraph skills	Does the paragraph have one main idea?										
	Does every sentence support the main idea of the paragraph?										
	Are the sentences logically related to one another?										
	Are the details/examples appropriate and relevant?										
	Total Number of *N*s for Category A:										
B. Sentence Skills	Are there sentences that demonstrate mastery of conjunctions (because, but, so)?										
	Are there correct, complete sentences only (no fragments)?										
	Are sentences elaborated with precise & content-based detail (answering the questions, for example, who, what, where, when and/or how)?										
	Are sentence starters varied? (Does at least one sentence begin with a subordinating conjunction such as "although" or "when")?										
	Total Number of *N*s for Category B:										

Adapted from Strategic inquiry: Starting small for big results in education (pp. 157–158), by Panero, N. S., & Talbert, J. E. (2013). Harvard Education Press. Copyright 2013 by the President and Fellows of Harvard College. Adapted with permission.

Appendix B

Sentence Tracker–Analyzing Student Baseline Writing Sample

Sentence Tracker - Indicates where to begin with sentences
1. Answer each of the following questions with a Yes (Y) or No (N) in the boxes below.
2. Count the number of N's and record (in the bottom row and right-hand column).
3. What patterns do you see? Who struggles most? What skills do students struggle with most?
4. Where will you begin and with whom (how might you adjust your target population)?

		Student 1	Student 2	Student 3	Student 4	Student 5	Student 6	Total N's per skill
Sentence Skills	1. Is there evidence of mastery of sentence boundaries (all complete sentences, no fragments or run-ons)?							
	2. Is there evidence of the ability to vary sentence types (for ex., use of question or exclamation)?							
	3. Is there evidence of mastery of use of the conjunctions but, because and so?							
	4. Is there evidence of mastery of the appositive (use of at least one appositive)?							
	5. Is there evidence of mastery of varied sentence starters (any sentences that begin with a subordinating conjunction, such as since, if, after, or although)?							
	6. Are sentences elaborated with rich detail answering questions such as who, when, how and why - beyond the bare minimum required for a simple sentence?							
	7. Is there varied, precise (content-specific, academic) vocabulary?							
	8. Is there evidence of mastery of mechanics (capitalization, punctuation, subject verb agreement, tense agreement, etc)?							
	Total N's per student:							

For Product Safety Concerns and Information please contact our EU
representative GPSR@taylorandfrancis.com
Taylor & Francis Verlag GmbH, Kaufingerstraße 24, 80331 München, Germany

www.ingramcontent.com/pod-product-compliance
Lightning Source LLC
Chambersburg PA
CBHW050637300426
44112CB00012B/1837